Melting Pot, Multiculturalism, and Interculturalism

Melting Pot, Multiculturalism, and Interculturalism

The Making of Majority-Minority Relations in the United States

Alfredo Montalvo-Barbot

LEXINGTON BOOKS
Lanham • Boulder • New York • London

Published by Lexington Books
An imprint of The Rowman & Littlefield Publishing Group, Inc.
4501 Forbes Boulevard, Suite 200, Lanham, Maryland 20706
www.rowman.com

6 Tinworth Street, London SE11 5AL, United Kingdom

Copyright © 2019 The Rowman & Littlefield Publishing Group, Inc.

All rights reserved. No part of this book may be reproduced in any form or by any electronic or mechanical means, including information storage and retrieval systems, without written permission from the publisher, except by a reviewer who may quote passages in a review.

British Library Cataloguing in Publication Information Available

Library of Congress Cataloging-in-Publication Data

ISBN 9781498591430 (cloth : alk. paper)
ISBN 9781498591454 (pbk : alk. paper)
ISBN 9781498591447 (electronic)

∞™ The paper used in this publication meets the minimum requirements of American National Standard for Information Sciences—Permanence of Paper for Printed Library Materials, ANSI/NISO Z39.48-1992.

Contents

Acknowledgments		vii
Introduction		1
1	Melting Pot, Pluralism, and Democracy	5
2	Minority Resistance: The Internal Colonization Argument	25
3	Decolonizing Education: The Ethnic Studies Movement	45
4	The Birth of Multiculturalism	63
5	Theorizing About Multiculturalism	77
6	Bridging Cultures: The Emergence of Interculturalism	93
Appendices		101
Bibliography		123
Index		129
About the Author		133

Acknowledgments

This book would not have been possible without the support of my family and colleagues. To my family in Puerto Rico, thank you for encouraging me in all of my pursuits and inspiring me to follow my dreams. Most importantly, I wish to thank my wife Fanny, my daughter Eileen, her husband Jarrod, and my lovely granddaughter Caroline for their support and inspiration. I want to thank the editorial staff at Lexington Books for their guidance and for helping me pull the book together.

Introduction

For most of my career as a college professor, I have followed, with great interest and intellectual curiosity, the meanings that Americans have given to ethnic and racial relationships in the United States. It is the primary purpose of this book to examine how and why the ideologies of melting pot, pluralism, multiculturalism, and more recently interculturalism have emerged and evolved. Specifically, I discuss how these ideologies have been legitimized, institutionalized, and challenged by activists, politicians, and intellectuals. The first chapter presents three interrelated ideological frameworks: melting pot, pluralism, and intercultural education. The melting-pot ideology emerged at a time when the dominance by Anglo-Saxons appeared to be under threat from the massive immigration of non-Anglo-Saxon southern Europeans, who were perceived by the Anglo-Saxons as being biologically and culturally unmeltable. By contrast, pluralists tried to solve the contradiction between forced assimilation and democracy by redefining racial relations. For pluralists, educating people in a democratic society meant recognizing and respecting the contribution of different ethnic groups to American society and culture. Programmatically, the intercultural relationships movement embraced the ideology of pluralism as an educational goal during the 1930s and 1940s and paved the way for the political effort to desegregate the school system. The intercultural education approach to race relations was primarily aimed at convincing and training White teachers and administrators in how to "attack the racial problem" in the school setting. This chapter examines a series of experimental projects designed to integrate the monoracial classrooms and schools. I have provided an overview of the different attempts to use the principles of pluralism in the education system to build intercultural tolerance and respect.

By the 1960s, the limits of applying pluralism to transforming intercultural relations had become evident. Specifically, it had become clear that training White people to recognize and respect the contribution of non-White people to mainstream culture was a necessary, but insufficient, step in building a culturally democratic society. Chapters 2 and 3 explore the resistance of minority groups to the assimilation process, and their dissatisfaction with the pluralistic ideology. Special consideration is given to the efforts by African Americans, Native Americans, and Latinos to define themselves, and to fight for equal representation in and through education. As dominant, White, middle-class intellectuals and politicians struggled to build a homogeneous, collective consciousness through education, ethnic minorities struggled to define and maintain their ethnic boundaries by demanding community-based control of the schools, as well as political and cultural autonomy.

As Chapter 3 shows, it was within the above context that the ethnic studies movement emerged and gained strength, during the late 1960s and early 1970s, as a tool for social change. In general, ethnic studies programs are designed around a single ethnic or racial group whose demands have forced the university administrators to create autonomous or semi-autonomous ethnic studies departments or schools. Many of these departments grant undergraduate or graduate majors or minors in their respective specialization. Ethnic studies programs are based on the assumption that ethnic identity and recognition in the classroom enhances minority students' self-esteem and academic achievement. Opponents of ethnic studies programs claim that ethnically-based education distorts the neutrality of teaching, keeps minority students away from the sciences and mathematics, and promotes academic segregation. This chapter provides data on the financial contribution of the Ford Foundation to ethnic studies programs. The data came from the Ford Foundation reports published on their website, and some of their printed reports. Noliwe M. Rooks and Fabio Rojas have reviewed some of these statistics in their research; however, I have included the Ford Foundation's contribution to Native American, Mexican American, and Puerto Rican studies to show that the Ford Foundation's involvement in Black studies reflects the Foundation's ideological and practical commitment to helping to address societal concerns and issues.

The emergence of the ideology of multiculturalism (along with diversity and inclusion) is examined in chapter 4. In his 1997 book, *We Are All Multiculturalists Now*, Nathan Glazer claimed that ". . . here in America, the word multiculturalism is a newcomer." Recently, in her book, *The Crisis of Multiculturalism in Europe*, Rita Chin (2017) traced the use of the noun "multiculturalism" to a 1957 report by the Modern Language Association in which the term was used to describe cultural diversity as socially enriching and engaging positively. This chapter provides a brief description of the emergence of the multicultural concept in public and scholarly debates, including Edward F. Haskell's 1941 novel, *Lance: A Novel About A Multicultural Man*, and the works of sociologists such as Everett V. Stonequist (marginal man), Louis Wirth (culture conflict), and Harry M. Shulman (culture and delinquency); however, in the 1970s, educators began to use the concept of multiculturalism to define the role of the school system in the process of building racial harmony in society. As originally conceived, multiculturalism represents an ideology that stresses the importance of introducing ethnic and racial topics into the existent curricula of schools, universities, and colleges to provide a more accurate examination and presentation of academic subjects. In many instances, multicultural courses are interdisciplinary, and they are coordinated through a specific office or committee. Despite their tactical and ideological differences, advocates of ethnic studies and multiculturalism share a concern for addressing the academic and intellectual needs of minority students, and for enriching the intellectual and academic experience of those involved in education; however, they also have had to face the charges of using education to promote ethnic and racial separatism and tribalism through indoctrination, and of distorting traditional knowledge. As with ethnic studies programs, multicultural education has been stereotyped as "affirmative action," promoting the use of "non-academic political criteria" for hiring and recruiting minority faculty and students. During the 1980s and 1990s, multiculturalism in education became the subject of political attack as well as philosophical and theoretical analysis outside the field of education.

Chapter 5 discusses how, by the mid-1980s, there had been a shift in emphasis from multicultural education as a "system-based product" to multicultural education as a "political process" linked to issues of individual and group identity. Outside academia, conservative politicians and journalists launched fierce attacks on multiculturalism by coupling issues of multiculturalism with the already controversial issues of political correctness and affirmative action. At a theoretical level, borrowing from the literature on postmodernism and liberation pedagogy, the school of critical multiculturalism stressed the need to empower teachers and students through a strategy of oppositional "discourse," whereby students and teachers had a legitimate voice to contest and criticize educational policies and practices.

Chapter 6 provides a brief introduction to the ideology of interculturalism. In 2010, German Chancellor Angela Merkel declared multiculturalism to be a complete failure. In her words, "Of course the tendency had been to say, 'let's adopt the multicultural concept and live happily side by side, and be happy to be living with each other.' But this concept [multiculturalism] has failed and failed utterly."[1] In France, Britain, Canada, and the United States, politicians expressed a similar view of multiculturalism. Some offered a pessimistic view of the political and cultural futures of their countries unless multicultural policies were replaced by assimilationist policies.[2] As explained in chapter 6, an alternative to multiculturalism was already in the making, namely, interculturalism. Interculturalism offers a new model for bridging the cultural divide and for overcoming the limitations of previous state-sponsored interracial and interethnic ideologies and programs. Interculturalism provides a holistic approach, where the concern is for encouraging open dialogue, based on trust, empathy, and mutual respect. Whether interculturalism can bridge the cultural divide, only time will tell!

NOTES

1. Kate Connolly, "Angela Merkel declares death of German multiculturalism." *The Guardian*, October 17, 2010. https://www.theguardian.com/world/2010/oct/17/angela-merkel-germany-multiculturalism-failures (accessed October 6, 2018). Author Ernesto Caravantes made a similar argument regarding multiculturalism in the United States in his 2010 book, *From Melting Pot to Witch's Cauldron: How Multiculturalism Failed America*.

2. Ibid., p. 9.

Chapter One

Melting Pot, Pluralism, and Democracy

The melting pot metaphor has shaped the imagination and aspirations of many Americans for many years. However, a metaphor is not just a way of defining reality; it also hides or ignores aspects of what it is intended to describe. The view of the United States as a melting pot can be traced back to 1782 when St. Jean de Crevecoeur, in his "Letters from An American Farmer," described the American society as a conglomerate of "individuals of all nations . . . melted into a new race of men, whose labours and posterity will one day cause great changes in the world."[1] However, Crevecoeur's melting pot metaphor did not go unchallenged. Italian Filippo Mazzei, a contemporary of Crevecoeur and who traveled to the United States during the late 1770s, accused Crevecoeur of misleading readers with his overgeneralizations, oversimplifications, and "ridiculous" ideas.[2] Instead, Mazzei portrays an American society full of racial and ethnic tensions struggling to survive and prosper. But Mazzei was in the minority, and by the early nineteenth century, the melting pot metaphor had deeply shaped the American mind. Intellectuals such as Ralph W. Emerson and Frederick J. Turner, and Henry James, celebrated the "prodigious amalgam . . . of racial ingredients" and the "cauldron of the great stew" forming the American society.[3]

Perhaps, it was Israel Zangwill's play *The Melting Pot* that contributed the most in popularizing the melting pot metaphor. Zangwill's play which opened in Washington, DC, in 1908, was received with enthusiasm, and "praised for its technical sophistication."[4] However, *The New York Times* called the play "insincere, unconvincing, cheap, tawdry, unimportant, and trash."[5]

> Mr. Zangwill is true neither to his Jews nor his Gentiles, though in the case of the former he does introduce occasional glimpses of customs and racial characteristics that are genuine enough and give the figures color. It may be doubted,

however, whether even he, with exceptional opportunity for studying the race, has ever seen a typical orthodox mother in Israel making merry on the Purim with an Irish housemaid as companion in the dance and a false nose to emphasize a racial trait. . . . Mr. Zangwill will stop at nothing to get a laugh . . . The "Melting Pot" is sentimental trash masquerading as a human document. That is the sum and substance of it.[6]

Similarly, *The Washington Post* questioned Zangwill's optimistic melting pot ideal: "However well Mr. Zangwill's play may be received for its artistic and dramatic qualities, it is to be feared that the doctrines he endeavors to preach will never become popular in this country."[7]

Like Crevecoeur's critics, those who questioned Zangwill's melting pot metaphor were reacting to the way in which immigrants from Southern and Eastern Europe were treated. Up to the mid-1800s, the immigrants coming to the United States were mainly English, Scotch, and Irish. By the late 1880s, however, immigration from the North and West of Europe began to decline and was followed by a significant increase in the migration of Southern and Eastern Europeans. In his influential book *Public Education in the United States: A Study and Interpretation of American Educational History* (1919), Ellwood P. Cubberley, a defender of the exclusionist Anglo-Saxon melting pot view, described Southern and Eastern European immigrants as follows:

These Southern and Eastern Europeans were of a very different type from the North and West Europeans who preceded them. Largely illiterate, docile, often lacking in initiative, and almost wholly without the Anglo-Saxon conceptions of righteousness, liberty, law, order, public decency, and government, their coming has served to dilute tremendously our national stock and to weaken and corrupt our political life. . . . The result has been that in many sections of our country foreign manners, customs, observances, and language have tended to supplant native ways and the English speech, while the so-called melting-pot has had more than it could handle. The new peoples, and especially those from the South and East of Europe, have come so fast that we have been unable to absorb and assimilate them, and our national life, for the past quarter of a century, has been afflicted with a serious case of racial indigestion.[8]

The melting pot exclusionists based their views on studies which allegedly demonstrated interracial differences in intelligence between Northern Europeans and Southern and Eastern Europeans. As Clifford Kirkpatrick puts it:

knowledge of group differences indicates where talent or defect is likely to be found, thus aiding individual selection. An opportunity to select immigrants from a group of Englishmen making application for admission would probably be more profitable than an opportunity to select immigrants from an equal number of Italians, of the average type that have been coming to this country in such great numbers.⁹

Kirkpatrick's study served to justify the Immigration Acts of 1917 and 1924, which imposed an English literacy test requirement on immigrants and limited the number of immigrants entering the country. In practice, these policies excluded Italians, Eastern European Hebrews, Bohemians, Slovaks, Bulgarians and others who were viewed by some as biologically and cognitively inferior and thus socially "unmeltable." In his book, *The Old World in the New: The Significance of Past and Present Immigration to the American People,* Edward A. Ross (1914) describes the inferiority of the new immigrants as follows:

> That the new immigrants are inferior in looks to the old immigrants may be seen by comparing, in a Labor Day parade, the faces of the cigar-makers and the garment-workers with those of the teamsters, piano-movers, and steam-fitters. Even aside from the pouring in of the ill-favored, the crossing of the heterogeneous is bound to lessen good looks among us. It is noteworthy that the beauty which has often excited the admiration of European visitors has shown itself most in communities of comparative purity of blood. New England, Virginia, and Kentucky have been renowned for their beautiful women, but not the commonwealths with a mixed population. It is in the less-heterogeneous parts of the Middle West, such as Indiana and Kansas, that one is struck by the number of comely women.¹⁰

Ross despised the "stupidity of the Slavs," "the Italian propensity toward violence," "the irresponsibility of the Irish," and "low character of the Hebrews" among many others. Further, he draws on Herbert Spencer's idea that the crossings of too-unlike races produce human beings with a chaotic constitution to explain what he assumes to be the biological superiority of the Anglo-Saxon American breed.

> The fusing of American with German and Scandinavian immigrants was only a reblending of kindred stocks, for Angles, Jutes, Danes, and Normans were 'wrought of yore into the fiber of the English breed. But the human varieties being collected in this country by the naked action of economic forces are too dissimilar to blend without producing a good many faces of a "chaotic constitution." Just as there is a wide difference in looks between Bretons and Normans, Dutch and Hanoverians, the Chinese of Hu-peh and the Chinese of Fukien, so broad contrasts in good looks may in time appear between the pure-blood parts of our country and those which have absorbed a motley assortment of immigrants.¹¹

Several commentators welcomed Ross's exclusionist reformulation of the melting pot for providing a "sound and compelling" argument for the restriction of the immigration of Southern Europeans.¹² The search for mechanisms to selectively control immigration continued throughout the early 1900s and produced a series of studies which supported the alleged mental superiority of the Nordic type.[13] One of the most notable of these was Bertha M. Boody's study, *A Psychological Study of Immigrant Children at Ellis Island* (1926). Her study paved the way to a view of immigration control which focused on differences within a group according to individual levels of intelligence, rather than national group identity. Critical of the use of "language" tests to measure the immigrant's fitness to stay in the country, Boody relied on a series of non-language drawing tests to measure the levels of intelligence among thirty-five immigrant children detained at Ellis Island between 1922 and 1924. Unlike the language-based tests, Boody's study of within and between racial group differences in intelligence found "nothing that sets one kind off from another . . ."[14] Consistent with previous studies, her policy recommendation consisted of reducing the number of immigrants arriving in America to assure a "more careful selection at the source . . . [and] the opportunity for more intensive physical and mental examination on arrival."[15]

AMERICANIZATION, PLURALISM, AND DEMOCRACY

At the same time that scientists struggled to discover genetic differences between ethnic groups, the spread of nationalism throughout Europe during World War I revitalized the Americanization movement under the auspice of politicians, educators, and social workers. One of the most influential leaders of the Americanization movement during this period was Frances A. Kellor; whose activism in favor of the legal and economic rights of immigrants led to her appointment as chief investigator in the Department of Labor of New York in 1910. Under her leadership, numerous town meetings, conventions, and programs took place aimed at protecting newly arrived immigrants from the "bare-faced robbery . . . and cold-blooded extortion and exploitation" by industrialists and by their compatriots.[16] Moreover, Kellor launched an attack on the level of injustice and indifference by the government which had left the welfare of the immigrants to "the padrone, the immigrant banker, the notary public, the saloon and to such associates as he may find or friendly welfare associations as he may chance upon."[17]

Based on her extensive research and activism Kellor concluded that a national Americanization plan was needed to solve the deplorable working and living conditions of the immigrants. In 1915, *The New York Times* announced Kellor's Americanization plan:

> Miss Frances A. Kellor, who managed the recent "Bundle Day" campaign, Commissioner of Immigration Howe and a number of others interested in immi-

grants organized the National Americanization Day Committee at 95 Madison Avenue yesterday. The committee plans a crusade against the "hyphen," and the immediate program calls for a novel celebration on July 4, at which a reception to new voters will be a feature in every large city. Miss Kellor said last night that the committee would try to have officials in all parts of the country adopt the Americanization plan . . . A prize of $250 has been offered for the best essay on "What America Means and How to Americanize the Immigrant."[18]

Unlike melting pot exclusionists, Kellor and the Americanization Day Committee were not "concerned with the question of eligibility for admission" of immigrants. Instead, they focused their attention on the Americanization of those who had passed the naturalization tests to ensure their loyalty to the United States.[19] On the Fourth of July 1915, all across the nation people celebrated Kellor's proposed Americanization Day. Civic leaders took the opportunity to remind newly naturalized Americans that "no man can bear allegiance to two countries . . . when the American Government gave your nationalization papers it gave you a new birth politically."[20] The assimilation message was clear: the economic and social welfare of the newly arrived immigrants depended not just on their capacity to assimilate to the American way of life, but also on the cohesion between native and foreign-born free from "racial animosities and bitter activities against each other."[21]

In contrast to the assimilationists, a group of scholars vehemently defended the right of immigrants to maintain their ethnic identity and advanced a pluralist view of society. Horace M. Kallen (1915), who introduced the notion of "cultural pluralism" in public debates, did not see any contradiction between Americanization and ethnically-based identity. In his words, "Americanization has not repressed nationality. Americanization has liberated nationality."[22]

> Immigrants appear to pass through four phases in the course of being Americanized. In the first phase, they exhibit economic eagerness, the greed of the unfed. Since external differences are a handicap in the economic struggle, they "assimilate," seeking thus to facilitate the attainment of economic independence. Once the proletarian level of such independence is reached, the process of assimilation slows down and tends to come to a stop . . . Then a process of dissimilation begins. The arts, life, and ideals of the nationality become central and paramount; ethnic and national differences change in status from disadvantages to distinctions. All the while the immigrant has been using the English language and behaving like an American in matters economic and political, and continues to do so. The institutions of the Republic have become the liberating cause and the background for the rise of the cultural consciousness and social autonomy of the immigrant Irishman, German, Scandinavian, Jew, Pole, or Bohemian.[23]

Scholar and journalist, Randolph S. Bourne (1916) took a similar position against forced Anglo-Saxon assimilation. In his view, "the early colonists . . . did not come to be assimilated in an American melting pot. They did not come to adopt the culture of the American Indian. They had not the smallest intention of giving themselves without reservation to the new country. They came to get freedom to live as they wanted to."[24]

The atmosphere of ethnic division became evident during the 1916 election as the American press reported a wave of "hyphenated votes," particularly of German-Americans whose patriotic alliance was highly questioned. However, they were not alone; there was widespread suspicion concerning the large body of foreign-born in the country.[25] Fear of discrimination and ethnic repression led many foreign-born residents, including Germans, to adopt American-sounding names and to formally and informally pledge allegiance to the United States. At the same time, state and local authorities repressed the use of the German language in the press and the schools. Some even suggested the creation of a scientific commission to study the "German type of mind" by using German prisoners as participants.

> It seems to be the popular belief that the German people are either suffering from a severe psychosis or they are racially defective. If either opinion be true, why not make an intensive study of some prisoners. . . . An expert psychological commission for this purpose might be appointed and put to work. If we find their mental state to be a hopeless, atavistic type . . . we may properly segregate them from contaminating the rest of mankind. . . .[26]

The American press frequently reported lynching incidents against German-Americans, forcing President Wilson to publicly call for an end to the wave of lynchings of suspected German American "enemies" and "negroes" that was spreading through the country. In his view, every lynching contributed to German anti-American lies and propaganda.[27] However, by the time the United States entered the war in 1917, the wave of political repression was widespread. Like Germans, Irish Americans came under suspicion due to the fear that their pro-independence stance regarding Ireland would undermine the United States' alliance with England against Germany.

At the same time, by the 1920s, pluralists had persuasively demonstrated that forced assimilation was not only politically and socially dangerous, but also inconsistent with democracy. A truly democratic society, they believed, is one in which differences in interests are protected, respected, and mutually interpenetrating.[28] Professor Julius Drachsler extensively examined the tension between democracy and inter-ethnic intolerance in his book *Democracy and Assimilation: The Blending of Immigrant Heritages in America*. Like many other scholars, Drachsler strongly believed that the European war "vigorously stimulated group-consciousness among the vast numbers of immigrants and to a degree among their immediate descendants. . . ."[29] Thus, there was the possibility that an internal war would be replicated in the United States between members of different European ethnic groups representing those countries engaged in the military conflict abroad: a possibility that became evident when European governments "consciously influenced their nationals in America to return and take part in the war."[30]

> Rioting between contending nationals broke out in various large immigrants centres. Protests were sent to Washington against discrimination in favor of French liners sailing with French reservists, whereas German and Austro-Hungarian vessels were not permitted to leave port with the reservists of those countries.[31]

Aware of the political danger of ethnic intolerance, Drachsler warned against stereotypical overgeneralization and urged for a pluralistic conception of immigration; one that would be consistent with democracy and individual rights.

> The groundwork of the civilization of the United States has been laid by pioneers of Anglo-Saxon blood. But since then, down to the present day, peoples of many lands and many stocks have added their share to the upbuilding of our culture, economic and non-material, thus proving by their works that they were capable of learning the spirit of American institutions and handing it down to their children. It is a curiously narrow view, one that lacks a long-range historical perspective and conceives of our civilization as fixed and unalterable, that does not interpret America's social development in this way. It magnifies and exaggerates the incompatibility of differing culture-values and by that very procedure tends to create the problem the introduction of which it dreads so much.[32]

Drachsler's advocacy of a pluralistic society was not without qualification, for he favored an immigration policy based on a scientific selection, distribution, and incorporation of the newcomers. His analysis of the limited data on intermarriage available led him to conclude that amalgamation through intermarriage is "not only not harmful but may even be desirable"[33] for it facilitates and accelerates cultural assimilation. Therefore, in his view, the fear of biological "mongrelization" should not influence immigration policies, but rather the regulation of immigration should be based on a scientific analysis of the economic needs of the country and the relative distribution of the different ethnic groups among the population. Although he realized the limitations of scientifically building a culture through immigration policies, he predicted that within a pluralistic society a natural amalgamation process would produce an organically integrated society.

> If, then, the experiment is to be ventured of consciously creating a composite culture in America, it can be approached only indirectly. By deliberately furthering an interest in the cultural achievements of the immigrant groups and by systematically bringing before the minds of their descendants these variegated culture-materials, a rich cultural environment or atmosphere might be created in which they would constantly move and find their spiritual expression. . . . Only as a result of these original apperceptions can a truly characteristic and organic composite culture be achieved . . . Its very essence is spontaneity.[34]

Drachsler's solution to the internal interracial conflict was for the public education system to create "the conditions under which the gifted individual will give free and unhampered expression to his native talent. . . . [Through] the conscious effort to marshal all the cultural contributions of the races and nations represented in the student-body, to bring these before the growing minds in a form easily grasped . . . to build up in them the attitude of intelligent and sympathetic insight into the life of diverse peoples."[35]

THE INTERCULTURAL RELATIONS MOVEMENT

To a great extent, World War I became a test case of the capacity of the American society and its institutions to maintain ethnic and racial stability. Within that context, improving intercultural relationships became a national priority among politicians and private organizations. In 1918 W. E. B. Du Bois called for Black people to put aside their "special grievances temporarily and to close ranks with their white fellow citizens" during the war period.[36] However, he advised that the "war would not be overcome until racial prejudice and injustice were overcome."[37] Influenced by W. E. B. Du Bois, during the 1920s, Rachel Davis DuBois, a social reformer and educator, developed and implemented "an assembly-program technique" for improving intercultural relationships within the school system in New Jersey and New York.[38] It consisted of assembly meetings composed of school staff, teachers, and administrators of different ethnic groups who met to discuss issues of racial and ethnic prejudice and discrimination and "to foster understanding and among the various culture groups in the U.S."[39] In 1934, she founded the Service Bureau for Intercultural Education (SBIE), a progressive and social reconstructionist organization dedicated to the development and dissemination of curricular material on value clarification and intercultural relationships.[40] William Heard Kilpatrick, chair of the SBIE in 1938 described intercultural education as follows:

> The word inter-cultural as here employed is now in accepted usage; it means much the same as inter-group and implies a scope that reaches beyond "race" to include also cultural differences. Intercultural education aims at the best possible achievement of the values of participation with, acceptance of, respect for others. It is an effort to bring education to bear as constructively as possible on actual and possible intercultural tensions and on the evils of any and all bias, prejudice, and discrimination against minority groups. In short, the effort of intercultural education is to ensure all the adequate realization of these values and to remove and cure the bias and prejudice leading to such discriminations.[41]

Politically, leaders of the SBIE shared a concern for the way prejudice and discrimination was undermining and contradicting democracy; a concern that shaped the political and intellectual climate during the 1930s and 1940s. SBIE members made the assumption that children have a natural tendency to live democratically, and that they learn to be prejudiced and to discriminate primarily through parents and peers. Therefore, it was the role of the school to help children build ethnic tolerance and "a clear understanding of what democracy means . . . and how democracy means respect for human personality wherever found."[42] From 1934 to 1939, the SBIE prepared a vast array of curricular material, delivered radio programs, and conducted numerous teacher in-service workshops for those who were interested in improving intercultural relationships in education and society. Its members strongly believed that educators have the responsibility for advancing the principles of democracy and ethnic tolerance through inter-cultural education.[43]

And, once again, the education system becomes an instrument of social change. The work of the Service Bureau for Intercultural Education (SBIE) gained momentum as politicians and experts tried to find ways of holding society together in light of the racial tension that prevailed in the United States. As John E. Walsh explains, "a number of forces and influences have come together in the final third of the twentieth century to make the development of a new theory of intercultural education both mandatory and urgent. Intercultural education itself is not something new; it is the post-World-War II emphasis on it which is new, spectacular, and profoundly revolutionary."[44]

The SBIE's strategy consisted of training teachers and administrators on how to identify and fix "maladjusted" students through intercultural education. In the words of William Heard Kilpatrick:

> Intercultural education must especially concern itself with all those personality maladjustments which foster and aggravate inter-group tensions. It must deal actively with maladjustments that lead a person to discriminate against members

of other groups, and also with the maladjustment which naturally follows from experiencing discrimination. When we consider the extent to which discrimination abounds in our midst, we can only marvel that the resulting maladjustments are no more numerous or serious.[45]

For Kilpatrick, "personality maladjustments" are the result of cumulative negative learning experiences such as humiliation, discrimination, and perceived unjust treatment. For the discriminated person, the effect of these experiences could manifest themselves in the form of an inferiority complex, resentment, and violence. However, those who discriminate also suffer from "maladjusted personality" as manifested in their superiority complex, their stereotyping, and prejudical attitudes. At the intergroup level, the maladjusted personality has the potential to foster scapegoating, that is, the tendency to transfer "a grudge or grievance . . . from the situation where it was built and take it out on some innocent third party or group."[46] Politically, the maladjusted personality represents the antithesis of American democracy, for it contradicts and threatens the principles of equality and justice.

By the late 1930s, the SBIE "intergroup assemblies" which started as experimental projects in New York were expanded to the entire country. With the assistance of the SBIE, in 1939 the Council Against Intolerance in America (CAIA), directed by William Warren Barbour, George Gordon Battle, and William Allen White, prepared and distributed about ten thousand copies of an anti-intolerance teaching manual to school districts across the country. The SBIE joined the CAIA's campaign by providing in-service training for teachers on the underlying philosophy of cultural democracy, and how to recognize and confront prejudices among their students.[47] The intercultural education program of the SBIE and the CAIA found public support from the First Lady Anna Eleanor Roosevelt, the National Council of Women of the United States, and prominent scholars such as Mortimer J. Adler, Albert Einstein, and Arthur H. Compton.[48]

The anti-intolerance movement extended its efforts throughout the 1950s. However, by the early 1960s, studies indicated that intergroup education "had been sorely neglected" in schools that were "located in industrial and suburban areas."[49] The two main factors accounting for the neglect, according to the studies, were the pressure for "crash programs in science and technology," and the lack of "teachers and administrators well qualified to advance intergroup education." Another indicator of the limitations and effectiveness of the intergroup education approach was the increasing racial and ethnic confrontations in the streets as militant minorities confronted prejudice and discrimination on their terms and conditions.

The pragmatic defense of democracy advocated by the SBIE program contrasted with the idealist position of intellectuals from the Great Books Movement for whom the center of the curriculum "must be the Classics, books contemporary in any age, permanent studies that draw out the elements of our common nature and link man to the best thought of the past."[50] Sociologist Henry Pratt Fairchild, in his 1947 book *Race and Nationality as Factors in American Life*, launched a strong attack on the pragmatic intercultural argument by claiming that

> two of the first, and most clearly justifiable, limitations of democracy that almost any country will make, take the form of distinctions between the native-born and the foreign-born, and between the citizen and the alien.[51]

In his view, these ethnic-based distinctions weaken the country's capacity to build a homogenous national identity. As he put it, "the United States has gone just about as far as it can safely go in permitting, in the name of humanitarianism and liberalism, the dilution of its own nationality."[52] In other words, by protecting the right of ethnic minorities to maintain their own identities, the United States had fallen into a profound interethnic division which could not be solved or controlled by "argument alone, nor by laws or any other form of coercion. The control must be self-control."[53]

THE BROWN DECISION: NOW IT'S 'HOW' AND 'WHEN'-NOT 'WHETHER'!

The intercultural programs and activities that emerged during the first four decades of the twentieth century were primarily aimed at changing the negative attitudes of the majority toward minority groups. It soon became evident that promoting peaceful coexistence between ethnic groups was a necessary but not sufficient approach to live up to the standards of a democratic society. A more permanent change in racial and ethnic attitudes and behaviors required a deeper intercultural understanding, that is, an appreciation for the contribution of every ethnic group to the mainstream society and culture as well as self-awareness of individual prejudices and racist conduct. One of the main impediments to achieving intercultural understanding was the *de facto* and the *de jure* segregation of the different ethnic groups. For cross-cultural understanding to develop, people of different ethnicities must have the opportunity to interact and learn from each other, even if these opportunities for intergroup interactions were judicially or legislatively mandated; this was the main goal of the Supreme Court decision in *Brown v. Board of Education of Topeka*.

Although the extra-legal rationale behind the *Brown* decision was to stop the detrimental psychological and social impact of school segregation on Black students, it was equally important in creating structural opportunities for intergroup relations that could lead to improved interracial relationships through social contact. However, the *Brown* decision and its enforcement caught many school administrators and staff across the country "unprepared" or "unwilling" to accommodate not only a large number of Black students coming into the system but also the large number of displaced Black teachers who worked in segregated schools. The magazine *Educational Leadership* dedicated its November 1955 issue to the topic of school desegregation, and in its editorial, titled "Now It's 'How' and 'When'—Not 'Whether,'" highlighted the spirit of emergency created by the *Brown* decision. The editorial sent an unequivocal message to educators:

> You individually have a responsibility for "how and "when" since you happen to be an educator and a citizen—free, any color and twenty-one plus. This is your problem. Maybe you didn't want it. It's yours notwithstanding.... On the issue of desegregation and integration, there can be no abdication of leadership responsibilities, no educational evasion.[54]

The opposition to the desegregation of the student body in schools and the tactics they used against desegregation have been extensively documented. *The Southern Manifesto*, produced by a group of separatists in Congress in 1956, denounced the *Brown* decision "as a clear abuse of judicial power" and decried "the Supreme Court's encroachment on the rights reserved to the States and to the people, contrary to established law, and to the Constitution."[55] By pledging to "use all lawful means to bring about a reversal of this decision" and to "prevent the use of force in its implementation," the *Manifesto* legitimized the ideological and practical opposition to the *Brown* decision. Some states approved laws and ordinances repealing compulsory school attendance, the closing of schools, and providing "public funds . . . as tuition grants for the private education of children in localities that abandoned public schools."[56] In 1963, the elected governor of Alabama, George Wallace, voiced the movement against school desegregation during his inaugural speech when he reiterated his vows "to disobey any federal court order" to enforce desegregation. Governor Wallace denounced the *Brown* decision as a communist threat to the constitutional right to freedom:

> This nation was never meant to be a unit of one...but a united of the many . . . each race, within its own framework has the freedom to teach . . . to instruct . . . to develop . . . to ask for and receive deserved help from others of separate racial stations. This is the great freedom of our American founding fathers . . . The true brotherhood of America, of respecting the separateness of others . . . has been so twisted and distorted from its original concept that there is a small wonder that communism is winning the world. We invite the negro citizens of Alabama to work with us from his separate racial station . . . as we will work with him

> . . . to develop, to grow in individual freedom and enrichment. We want jobs and a good future for both races . . . the tubercular and the infirm. This is the basic heritage of my religion . . . for we are all the handiwork of God. But we warn those, of any group, who would follow the false doctrine of communistic amalgamation that we will not surrender our system of government . . . our freedom of race and religion . . . that freedom was won at a hard price and if it requires a hard price to retain it . . . we are able . . . and quite willing to pay it.[57]

The implementation of the *Brown* decision did not benefit all Black people equally. Many Black teachers who lost their jobs in the previously segregated schools and who White school administrators deemed incompetent to teach in integrated schools, found themselves unemployed or underemployed.

> S. P. Portis, superintendent of schools at Hamburg in southern Arkansas, said what others across the South have said: Negro teachers are not as competent as whites. The Negro teachers come from culturally deprived homes, inferior public schools and second-rate teachers college. Mr. Portis suggested that a whole new generation of Negro teachers might have to be trained through desegregated public schools and colleges before they would be ready in appreciable numbers to enter the previously all-white schools.[58]

Allegations of violation of the Civil Rights Act of 1964 in the school system led the National Education Association in 1965 to conduct a study which shed some light on the discrimination facing Black teachers under the school desegregation plan:

> As has been demonstrated, "white schools" are viewed as having no place for Negro teachers. As a result, when Negro pupils in any number transfer out of Negro schools, Negro teachers become surplus and lose their jobs. It matters not whether they are as well qualified as, or even better qualified than other teachers in the school system who are retained. Nor does it matter whether they have more seniority. They were not employed as teachers for the school system . . .[59]

Overall, the investigation revealed a series of strategies employed at newly desegregated schools that kept Black administrators and teachers out of the school system. When schools were integrated through consolidation, principals were demoted, and Black teachers were assigned to "specialty types of limited contact positions such as elementary school librarian, counselor, special education teachers, and coach." In some Southern counties, legislation was passed close to the initial stage in the desegregation process which deprived some teachers of their right to tenure. This tactic allowed for the dismissal of teachers who advocated for desegregation. It was also documented the discriminatory use of the National Teacher Examination procedure by increasing the average passing score, the closing of desegregated trade schools, and the revocation of teaching certificates upon the closing of the schools. In other states, anti-integration laws allowed the state to close "nine [all-White] schools in three communities and the displacement of 12,700 pupils." This action was a response to the demand by the states to desegregate the school faculty by fully integrating displaced Black teachers. In the Southern region of Atlanta school districts were reluctant to desegregate the schools (only 604 out of the 2,220 districts had been desegregated by 1965) and "none of the districts contemplated faculty desegregation . . . beyond integrated faculty meetings."[60]

FACILITATING INTERCULTURAL RELATIONS IN DESEGREGATED SCHOOLS

Two significant reports prepared in the 1970s illustrate the desperation and creativity among education experts dealing with school desegregation during the years that followed the *Brown* decision. In 1970 the University of Missouri's School of Education and Division for Continuing Education published a resource booklet which described twenty-two projects implemented in the Kansas City metropolitan area to "attack" the "problem of multi-racial classrooms."[61] The projects emphasized planning skills, cooperative relations, communications and decision making. Appendix A summarizes some of the twenty-two projects in the study. As the table indicates, the main emphasis of these projects was the preparation of the staff, teachers, and White students to learn about Black history and culture, and to eliminate or reduce their prejudice against Blacks. Concerning procedure, some projects used a minimalist approach by including particular material or units into the regular curriculum, typically in the history, literature, and music courses. Despite their noble intention of raising students' awareness of the contribution of minorities to the larger society, these projects had the potential to be perceived as "just plugging in" related facts to offer a token contribution in an effort to create better human relations.[62] Other projects used a combination of role-playing, sociometry, dialect analysis, ethnic-based puzzles, and pictographic and audio-visual material. These interactive techniques were geared toward helping White students experience and reject prejudice and discrimination. To identify and attack the problems of prejudice and discrimination among teachers, some of the projects included some form of voluntary in-service training on intergroup relationships, prejudice reduction workshops, counseling, and group discussions on reading material dealing with racial topics. The evaluation of these approaches indicates that in many cases it was difficult to motivate teachers to participate in these projects voluntarily.

Overall, the intercultural projects were based on the assumption that prejudice and discrimination "are the result of misinformation or incomplete information."[63] Therefore, by giving the correct information to the participants, they will correct their prejudices and discriminatory attitudes and practices. However, the program evaluation showed that the "filtering" effect hampered the effectiveness of the "re-learning" approach to reducing prejudice. The researchers found that the "social pressures or personal feelings of inadequacy on the part of the individual serve as a filter when new information is provided. His filter system repels data which would show the prejudice to be untrue, but it permits information to pass which support the prejudice."[64]

A second study conducted by The Western Regional School Desegregation Projects (WRSDP) in California reported discouraging news regarding school desegregation. The WRSDP had identified a series of barriers to effective desegregation and integration. First, some of the citizens who favored desegregation and integration "advocated it for others only as they move to ex-urban areas or to private schools."[65] Second, in many school districts, there was a lack of institutional financial commitment to invent, implement, and maintain new integration programs. Third, most educators lacked adequate preparation and skills to deal with new patterns of race relations in school. Finally, some parents and community residents resisted desegregation and busing for fear of the Black Power movement, fear of increasing mixed marriages, and the potential of interracial violence. According to the report, these and other underlying, unresolved feelings about desegregation prompted the "flight of Whites and merchants from town."[66] All across the country, desegregation advocates faced the challenge of developing strategies to address the anger, frustration, and confusion that plagued local communities, and that exacerbated racial tension.

In response to the increasing resistance against desegregation, in 1971 the WRSDP offered a series of training courses for those in charge of directing the integration of the school systems in California and other areas of the Southwest to raise their awareness about the legal consequences of noncompliance with the *Brown* decision (see appendix B). For instance, in one of the sections the trainers, using *Mendez et al. v. Westminster School District, et al.*,[67] presented the group a school desegregation order under which the participants had sixteen hours to take action and to provide a rationale for compliance or for their failure to comply with the order. A second approach involved identifying forces in favor of and against desegregation within the local community. The relative strength of these forces was diagnosed, and the information was used to develop a plan for change. A more comprehensive strategy consisted of establishing lines of communication and action between community-based organizations, such as the Mexican-American Legal Defense and Educational Fund, and the NAACP, to advance the desegregation plan.

NOTES

1. John Hector St. John Crevecoeur, "Letters from An American Farmer," (ed.) Giles Gunn, *New World Metaphysics: Readings on the Religious Meaning of the American Experience.* (New York: Oxford University Press) 1981, p.135–134.

2. Filippo Mazzei, *Political and Historical Research on the United States of America.* (Charlottesville: University Press of Virginia), [1788] 1979.

3. Henry James, *The American Scene* (Indiana: Indiana University Press, 1968) p. 130.

4. Israel Zangwill, *The Melting Pot* (New York: Macmillan), 1909. Among other things, the play tells the story of David Quixano, a Russian Jewish man who falls in love with Vera, a Russian Christian woman. Together they struggle to overcome the animosity arising from their cultural differences. During his conversation with Vera, David expresses his desire to compose a symphony that would express his dream of an American society free of ethnic divisions and hatred. It is at this point that he expresses the extensively quoted description of America as God-made: ". . . the great Melting-Pot where all the races of Europe are melting and re-forming . . . Germans and Frenchmen, Irishmen and Englishmen, Jews and Russians—into the Crucible with you all!"

5. "New Zangwill Play Cheap and Tawdry," *The New York Times*, September 7, 1909, p. 9.

6. Ibid., p. 9. See also, *The New York Times*, "A Spread-Eagle Play by Israel Zangwill: The Melting Pot" Insincere as a Work of Art and Unconvincing as a Human Document." September 12, 1909, p. 10.

7. "The Alien's Opportunity" *The Washington Post*, Oct 7, 1908. pg. 6.

8. Ellwood P. Cubberley, *Public Education in the United States: A Study and interpretation of American Educational History* (Boston: Houghton Mifflin, 1919[1947]), pp. 482–488. Like many other scholars of his time, Cubberley realized the importance of education, religion, and work as assimilationist tool. However, he was convinced that the "melting-pot" had reached its maximum capacity, therefore, the assimilation of the foreign-born will require two or three generations, and the "amalgamation of the descendants of these peoples into our evolving American racial stock may take place through intermarriage and the mixture of blood," p. 488.

9. Clifford Kirkpatrick, *"Intelligence and Immigration."* (Baltimore: Williams & Wilkins, 1926), p. 105.

10. Edward A. Ross, *The Old World in the New: The Significance of Past and Present Immigration to the American People* (New York: The Century, Co, 1914), p. 288.

11. Ibid., pp. 288–289.

12. See Y. S., "Book Review," *The Mississippi Valley Historical Review* Vol. 1, No.3, Dec., 1914, pp. 454–455; J. P. Lichtenberger, "Book Review," *Annals of the American Academy of Political and Social Science*, Vol. 58, March 1915, pp. 256–257.

13. For a complete review of these studies see, Bertha M. Boody, *A Psychological Study of Immigrant Children at Ellis Island.* (Baltimore: Williams and Wilkins Company) 1926.

14. Ibid., p. 120.

15. Ibid., p.157.

16. "Important Work in Good Hand," *The New York Times*, October 7, 1910.

17. Frances A. Kellor, "Justice for the Immigrant," *Annals of the American Academy of Political and Social Science*, Vol. 52, March 1914, p. 160.

18. "Make Americans on July 4," *The New York Times*, May 26, 1915.

19. "Important Work in Good Hands," *The New York Times*, October 7, 1910.

20. "Clark Asks Loyalty of New Americans," *The New York Times*, July 5, 1915. See also *The Washington Post*, "One Flag for Aliens," February 23, 1916.

21. Frances A. Kellor, "Immigration and the Future," *Annals of the American Academy of Political and Social Science*, Vol. 93, January 1921, p. 210.

22. Horace M. Kallen, "Democracy Versus the Melting Pot: A Study of American Nationality." *The Nation*, February 18, 1915, Vol. 100, No. 2590. p. 190.

23. Ibid., p.190.

24. Randolph S. Bourne, "Trans-National America," *The Atlantic Monthly*, July 1916, Vol. 118, p. 91.

25. "Wisconsin Hinges on the Hyphen Vote," *The New York Times*, October 26, 1916, p. 6. See also, *The New York Times*, "A German-American Speaks: The Fiction of an Alien Vote in the Middle West." August 1, 1915, p. 6.

26. L. Pierce Clark, "To study German Minds: A Commission to Work With Prisoners is Suggested." *The New York Times*, April 5, 1918, p. 14.

27. "President Demands That Lynching End," *The New York Times*, July 27, 1918, p. 7.

28. John Dewey, *Democracy and Education*, (New York: Macmillan Company), 1916, p. 100–101. Julius Drachsler refers to this form of political organization as "cultural democracy." See also Julius Drachsler, *Democracy and Assimilation* (New York: Macmillan Company), 1920, p. 215.

29. Julius Drachsler, *Democracy and Assimilation: The Blending of Immigrant Heritages in America.* (New York: Macmillan Company), 1920, p. 7.

30. Ibid., p. 12.

31. Ibid., p. 12.

32. Julius Drachsler, "The Scientific Regulation of Immigration," *Proceedings of the Academy of Political Science in the City of New York*, January 1924, Vol. 10, No. 4. p. 120.

33. Ibid., p. 151.
34. Ibid., p. 151, p. 187.
35. Ibid., p. 189.
36. Mark Ellis, "Closing Ranks and Seeking Honors: W. E. B. Du Bois in World War I," *The Journal of American History*, June 1992, Vol. 79, No. 1. p. 99.
37. Friends Historical Library of Swarthmore College. "An Inventory of the Rachel Davis DuBois Papers, 1920–1993." http://www.swarthmore.edu/Library/friends/ead/5035dubo.xml (accessed May 18, 2011).
38. Rachel Davis DuBois (1892–1993) "was born into a Quaker family in Salem County, New Jersey, the daughter of C. Howard and Bertha Haines Davis. She earned a degree in natural science at Bucknell University, PA, in 1914. She was active throughout her long life initiating and maintaining numerous projects and conferences to promote intercultural and interfaith understanding, shaping the field of intercultural education through her teaching and conferences, corresponding with a long list of friends and associates, writing articles and books, and much more. She worked closely with the New York Friends Center and Earlham College, as well as the Southern Christian Leadership Conference and major Jewish groups. She was a pioneer in inter-faith and inter-racial dialogue and intercultural education and traveled all over the U.S. and abroad to share her programs with other communities." http://www.swarthmore.edu/Library/friends/ead/5035dubo.xml (accessed December 15, 2008).
39. Shafali Lal, "1930s Multiculturalism: Rachel Davis DuBois and the Bureau for Intercultural Education," *Radical Teacher*, May 2004, No. 69, p. 18.
40. The SBIE had three theoretical orientations: social reconstructionism, which proposes that the curriculum should be based on social reality; the child-centered approach with its emphasis on the needs and interests of the child for curriculum development; and values clarification progressivism, which puts the emphasis on the importance of value-laden curricular content. (See, Peter A. Sola, "Intercultural Education," in *Encyclopedia of African-American Education*, ed. Faustine C. Jones-Wilson, Charles A. Asbury, Margo Okazawa-Rey, D. Kamili Anderson, Sylvia M. Jacobs, Michael Fultz. (CT: Greenwood Press) 1996, p. 229–230.
41. William Heard Kilpatrick, "Basic Principles in Intercultural Education," in *Intercultural Attitudes in the Making: Parents, Youth Leaders, and Teachers at Work.* Ed. William Heard Kilpatrick and William Van Til. (New York: Harper and Brothers) 1947, p. 4.
42. Ibid., p. 5.
43. Shafali Lal, "1930s Multiculturalism," p. 19.
44. John E. Walsh, *Intercultural Education in the Community of Man*, (HI: The University Press of Hawaii) 1973, p. 1.
45. William Heard Kilpatrick, "Basic Principles in Intercultural Education," p. 15.
46. Ibid., p. 15.
47. "Schools in War on Propaganda: Educators Unite to Combat Growing Intolerance in Country," *The New York Times,* August 6, 1939, p. D5.
48. "79 Leaders Unite to Aid Democracy: Men of Science, Philosophy and Religion Issue Call to Safeguard Our Freedom." *The New York Times*, June 1, 1940, p. 10.

49. "Stress on Science for Pupils Scored: Intergroup Education Found to be Sorely Neglected in 2 Studies by Jewish Unit." *The New York Times*, January 19, 1960, p. 6.

50. Cecil H. Driver and Myres S. McDougal, "Review of The Higher Learning in America," by Robert Maynard Hutchins, *The Yale Law Journal* 46, no. 8 (June 1937), p. 1433.

51. Henry Pratt Fairchild, *Race and Nationality as Factors in American Life* (NY: Ronald Press Company) 1947, p.148.

52. Ibid., p. 202.

53. Ibid., pp. 205–206.

54. William Van Til, "Now It's 'How' and 'When'—Not 'Whether." *Educational Leadership*. November. 1955, Vol. 13, No. 2.

55. "The Southern Manifesto," *Congressional Record*, 84th Congress Second Session. Vol. 102, part 4 (March 12, 1956). Washington, DC: Governmental Printing Office, 1956. 4459–4460. http://www.strom.clemson.edu/strom/manifesto.html (accessed December 15, 2008).

56. "Virginia Now Facing Hard School Decision: Choice Between Some Integration and No Schools Appears Near," *The New York Times*, November 30, 1958, p. E7.

57. "The 1963 Inaugural Address of Governor George C. Wallace" January 14, 1963 Montgomery, Alabama http://www.archives.state.al.us/govs_list/inaugural speech.html (accessed December 15, 2008).

58. "Rights Act Forces School Equality: Many Districts in The South Comply to Get U.S. Aid." *The New York Times*, June 27, 1965, p. 22.

59. National Education Association, *Report of Task Force Survey of Teacher Displacement in Seventeen States*, (Washington, DC: National Education Association), 1965, p. 23.

60. "Rights Act Forces School Equality," *The New York Times*, June 29, 1965, p. 22.

61. Joseph P. Caliguri (ed.), *Suburban Interracial Education Projects: A Resource Booklet*. (Missouri: School of Education and Division for Continuing Education, University of Missouri, Kansas City) 1970.

62. Ibid., p. 56.

63. R. Murray Thomas, *Social Class Differences in the Classroom: Social Class, Ethnic and Religious Problems*, (New York: David McKay Company), 1965, p. 72.

64. Ibid., p. 72.

65. Mark Chesler. *Preparing for School Desegregation: A Training Program for Intergroup Educators*, Vol.1, June 1972, p. 11–12. https://files.eric.ed.gov/fulltext/ED064460.pdf (accessed December 12, 2008).

66. Ibid., p. 18.

67. *Mendez, et al v. Westminster School District, et al*, 64 F.Supp. 544 (C.D. Cal. 1946), aff'd, 161 F.2d 774 (9th Cir. 1947). In this case, which challenged racial segregation in Orange County, California schools, the United States Court of Appeals for the Ninth Circuit held that the segregation of Mexican and Mexican American students into separate Mexican schools was unconstitutional.

Chapter Two

Minority Resistance: The Internal Colonization Thesis

African-Americans: International and National Colonization

The melting pot metaphor shaped the imagination and aspirations of many Americans for many years. However, a metaphor is not just a way of defining reality; it also hides or ignores aspects of what it is intended to describe. As I discuss in this chapter, those excluded from the melting pot metaphor relied on a colonial analogical perspective or metaphor to define and confront their reality. Minority resistance to forced assimilation during the 1930s and 1940s often involved open confrontation with state authority, which leaders of radical organizations, such as the Black Panther and the Black Power Movement, described as a colonial apparatus of oppression similar to those of colonial regimes in third-world countries. Hence, many Black people became suspicious of any attempts by the government or private organizations to solve inter-racial tension without addressing the root cause of the problem, namely, the internal colonization of minority people in the United States.

Even though in 1941 President F. D. Roosevelt issued Executive Order 8802, banning racial discrimination in defense industries and the government job discrimination against Blacks and other minorities continued throughout the 1940s and 1950s. Rural Blacks who moved to the cities in search for jobs in the military industries had to compete with Whites for jobs fearlessly, and positions, as well as for housing accommodations, particularly in predominantly white neighborhoods. This competition became the source of violent confrontations between both groups. In Indiana, for instance, where in 1943 about twelve percent of the population was Black, racially-based clashes increased between already established Blacks and the newly arrived "white workers . . . coming from the hill sections of Kentucky and Tennessee." The clashes occurred in "street car and bus line . . . and movie theatres" which had been opened to Blacks for fear of lawsuits under Indiana anti-discriminatory laws.[1]

Economically-based clashes between Blacks and Whites became a common occurrence in industrial cities in Ohio and Detroit.

Meanwhile, in Chicago and New York City, members of the National Urban League (NUL) worked devoutly to prevent and contain minor racial incidents that could lead to racial riots among workers and the youth. The NUL launched the "Better Behavior Campaign" as an effort to stop and neutralize the potential effect of rumors and reports of "discrimination against Negroes" in the armed forces and military industries. According to the NUL, these rumors and reports, "whether factual or fanciful" were feeding the anger and frustration of the youth. As Earl B. Dickerson, president of the Chicago Urban League told the press, "Let one of those stories be told in a pool room or a night spot on the South Side, within the moment the whole place is roaring with load talk, expressions of resentment and downright threats and disorder."[2] City leaders and civic organizations have learned a lesson from the violent riot that started at the Belle Isle Park in Detroit and spread to other city neighborhoods on June 20, 1943.

> A sudden fist fight touched it off, sent fighting, cursing whites and Negroes battling over the bridge, spilling through the city. Like wildfire, the rioting spread to "Paradise Valley," Detroit's downtown Negro section, washed over Woodward Avenue, Detroit's main street. Gangs of whites and Negroes roved the streets, smashing windows, tipping cars, looting stores, seizing guns and ammunition in pawnshops. Courageously Negro leaders toured the Valley in sound cars. But their pleas for peace were drowned by jeers. . . . Finally, after a proclamation by Franklin Roosevelt ordering the rioters to disperse, Federal troops marched in, cleared the streets. After 24 nightmarish hours, Detroit was quieted down, counted the toll of one of the worst riots in modern history U.S. history: at least 23 dead, over 700 injured, over 600 jailed. Of the Negroes, police had shot at least eight.[3]

Meanwhile, leaders of the Civil Rights Movement, although not oblivious to the racial tension in the North, concentrated their efforts upon the eradication of Jim Crow laws and segregation in the South. The NAACP's strength was evidenced in *Shelley v. Kraemer* (1948) in which Supreme Court declared unconstitutional the "judicial enforcement of restrictive covenants" as a legal tool to deprive people of the right to own or rent property.[4] Another major victory was the 1954 Supreme Court *Brown* decision. The decision mandated an end to school segregation by overturning the "separate but equal" precedent established in the 1896 Supreme Court ruling in *Plessy v. Ferguson*. In *Brown*, the court held that state-mandated segregated public schools deprive black children of access to equal educational opportunities.[5] Outside the court, the Civil Rights Movement obtained federal protection for the voting rights of Black people under the "existing civil voting statute . . . [which]

declares that all citizens who are otherwise qualified to vote at any election (state or federal) shall be entitled to exercise their vote without distinction of race or color."[6]

The *Brown* decision not only expanded educational and social opportunities for minorities but also provided a fertile ground to initiate institutional changes. Many minority members who became integrated within the education system brought with them or later on acquired the radical discourse produced by national and international radical leaders who denounced colonial oppression around the world. The United Nation's efforts at eliminating colonial regimes around the world created an atmosphere of optimism for ethnic minorities in developed countries whose struggle with racism has been largely ignored at the international level. As early as 1945 appellate court Judge Henry Edgerton, in dissent, used the United Nations' call for respect for human rights to oppose the validity and enforcement of the segregating housing restrictive covenants which prevented Blacks from owning properties in White neighborhoods.[7] In so doing, Judge Edgerton elevated Jim Crow segregationist system to an international level and put race relations in the United States under the scrutiny of the rest of the world.

Similarly, in 1947, the NAACP issued *An Appeal to the World: A statement on the denial of Human Rights to minorities in the case of citizens of Negro Descent in the United States and An Appeal to the United Nations for Redress*.[8] The document, prepared by W. E. B. Du Bois and other NAACP members, provided a historical analysis of racism in the United States and its detrimental effect on democracy. The NAACP stated that the federal government had

> continually cast its influence with imperial aggression throughout the world and withdrawn its sympathy from the colored peoples and from small nations. It has become through private investment a part of the imperialistic bloc which is controlling the colonies of the world.[9]

According to the NAACP, the enemy of the United States was not Russian communist expansionism, but the federally-supported racist regime that had prevailed in the country for decades. The appeal internationalized the fight for racial equality in the United States.

By the 1950s and 1960s, scholars and political activists had adopted the United Nations' anti-colonialist agenda to frame the reality of ethnic minorities within industrialized societies. The presentation of Blacks as colonized people can be traced back to the First World Conference of Negro Writers and Artists celebrated in Paris in 1956. At that meeting "black Americans spontaneously considered their problems from the standpoint as their fellow Africans."[10] Black Americans at the meeting believed that they shared a common history of White colonization and oppression with Blacks in Africa, the Caribbean, and Latin America. However, as Frank Fanon indicates the conference made Black Americans aware of the particularities of their problems.

> The only common denominator between the blacks from Chicago and the Nigerians or Tanganyikans was that they all defined themselves in relation to the whites. But once the initial comparisons had been made and subjective feelings had settled down, the black Americans realized that the objective problems were fundamentally different.[11]

Upon their return to the United States, the participants formed the American Society of African Culture and began publishing the quarterly journal *Forum*. Its editor, John A. Davis, described the philosophy of the journal as follows:

> We believe that a good society can be rationally developed, that it is based on the dignity of man and the rule of law, that it requires the political consensus of all people, that it must provide economic and social mobility for its citizens on the basis of their ability, that it permits, a personal choice in the spending of the fruits of man's toil and that it provides for political stability and the orderly transfer of political power.[12]

The statement "the orderly transfer of political power" reveals the organization's view of Blacks as colonized people and their future liberation and decolonization. The view of ethnic minorities as colonized and oppressed people and the internationalization of the American problem of racism shaped public policies and research dealing with ethnic and racial relations in the United States. Acts of civil disobedience and violence led to legal reforms such as the 1954 *Brown* decision on school desegregation, the enactment of The Civil Rights Act of 1964, which outlawed racial segregation in schools, public places, and employment, and The Voting Rights Act of 1965. These and other anti-segregation legislation enacted during the 1960s were intended to "rescue the Negro from inferior status" and "to reach the official caste system . . . to get rid of it."[13]

Regarding research, for decades Gunnar Myrdal's *An American Dilemma: The Negro Problem and Modern Democracy* remained as one of the most influential studies guiding public policy. The study helped debunk the social-Darwinist views of scholars such as William G. Sumner and Robert Park.

> Sumner could not fail to have a particularly strong influence on social science thinking about the problems of the South and, specifically, about the Negro problem. The theory of "folkways" and "mores" has diffused from the scientists and has in the educated classes of the South become a sort of regional political *credo*. The characterization of something as "folkways" or "mores" or the

stereotype that "stateways cannot change folkways"—which under no circumstances can be more than a relative truth—is used in the literature on the South and on the Negro as a general formula of mystical significance.[14]

Moreover, the study points out that ". . . occasionally the do-nothing (*laissez-faire*) implications of Park's assumptions are revealing: The races of high visibility, to speak in naval parlance, are the natural and inevitable objects of race prejudice."[15] In Park's view, social equilibrium emerges out of a natural and *laissez-faire* process of racial accommodation with its concomitant disappearance of race consciousness. By contrasts, the center of the racial tension in America, according to the Myrdal report,

> is the moral dilemma of the American—the conflict between his moral valuations on various levels of consciousness and generality. The "American Dilemma" . . . is the ever-raging conflict between, on the one hand, the valuations preserved on the general plane which we shall call the "American Creed," where the American thinks, talks, and acts under the influence of high national and Christian precepts, and, on the other hand, the valuations on specific planes of individual and group living, where personal and local interests; economic, social, and sexual jealousies; considerations of community prestige end conformity; group prejudice against particular persons or types of people; and all sorts of miscellaneous wants, impulses, and habits dominate his outlook.[16]

The resolution of this dilemma and the solution to the racial problems facing the United States demand not just economic reforms but also cultural and political changes. Specifically, the racial conflict was not a Negro problem but a White problem; that is, it is a problem produced by "what is in White people's mind."[17] Hence, the solution to the conflict demands changes in the way White people think, their values and beliefs regarding Blacks and other minorities. Myrdal suggests that this cultural transformation, although slow, already was in its initial stage of development.

> The white man is . . . in the process of losing confidence in the theory which gave reason and meaning to his way of life. And since he has not changed his life much, he is in a dilemma. This change is probably irreversible and cumulative. It is backed by the American Creed. The trend of psychology, education, anthropology, and social science is toward environmentalism in the explanation of group differences, which means that the racial beliefs which defended caste are being torn away.[18]

On the other hand, Myrdal predicted an increase in the militancy of Blacks due to the growing bitterness produced by White discrimination within a culture that paradoxically promotes democracy and equalitarian values.

> The Negro spirit is rising, spurred by the improvement in education. The Negro group is being permeated by the democratic and equalitarian values of the American culture. Since at the same time there has been increasing separation between the two groups, Negroes are beginning to form a self-conscious "nation within the nation," defining ever more clearly their fundamental grievances against white America. America can never more regard its Negroes as a patent, submissive minority. Negroes will continually become less well "accommodated." They will organize for defense and offense. They will be more and more vociferous. They will watch their opportunities ever more keenly. They will have a powerful tool in the caste struggle against white America: the glorious American ideals of democracy, liberty, and equality to which America is pledged . . . The Negroes are a minority, and they are poor and suppressed, but they have the advantage that they can fight wholeheartedly. The whites have all the power, but they are split in their moral personality. Their better selves are with the insurgents. The Negroes do not need any other allies.[19]

Finally, the international pressure for putting an end to imperialism and for the spreading of democracy around the world will require that the United States "demonstrate to the world that American Negroes can be satisfactorily integrated into its democracy."[20]

The publication of *An American Dilemma* in 1944 was followed by a series of theories explaining inner-city violence behavior from different perspectives which did little to challenge the establishment. For instance, Albert Reiss (1951) attributed antisocial behavior to failure of personal and social control, Albert Cohen (1955) claimed that antisocial behavior was a form of protest against the middle class cultural measuring rod, Robert Merton (1957) and Richard Cloward and Lloyd Ohlin (1960), linked minority antisocial behavior to the disjunction between culturally defined goals and socially acceptable means and the lack of opportunities to succeed in society. Gresham M. Sykes and David Matza (1957) saw antisocial behavior as being sustained by a "subterranean value system" that allows deviants to drift between conventional and illegitimate conduct.

SOCIOLOGY, MOBILIZATION, AND REFORM

Federal and local officials remained puzzled by what seems to an unsolvable problem: inner-city minority unrest. The most ambitious program that integrated some of the main sociological theoretical insights of the 1950s and early 1960s was the New York City 1961 Mobilization for Youth (MOBY) program. This community empowerment program was aimed at getting the youth and their parents involved in solving some of the social problems affecting their communities such as tenancy physical and legal conditions, voter registration, and crime.

Four years after MOBY was launched, sociologist Kenneth B. Clark and the Harlem Youth Opportunities Unlimited team (HAYOU) published *Youth in the Ghetto: A Study of the Consequences of Powerlessness and a Blue Print for Change.* For the HAYOU team, the social, political, and economic conditions in Harlem compared to those found in colonial societies.

> Even in a cursory examination of the power potentials in the Harlem community reveals that there are few, if any, examples of primary and consistent power in the hands of resident individuals and groups. The community can best be described in terms of the analogy of a powerless colony. Its political leadership is divided, and all but one or two of its political leaders are shortsighted and dependent upon the larger political power structure. Its social agencies are financially precarious and dependent upon sources outside the community. Its churches are isolated or dependent. Its economy is dominated by small businesses which are largely owned by absentee owners, and its tenements and other real property are also owned by absentee landlords.[21]

Based on a series of experimental projects conducted by the HAYOU the researchers made a set of policy recommendations to empower the community, including job training for young people, community control of the schools, community leadership training, and culture building programs. The proposal for community-based control of the school system was justified on the demographic pattern of the school system in New York.

> By the 1960s fewer than 50 percent of the students enrolled in New York's public schools were white; almost a third were black, and the rest were presumably "Hispanic" (largely Puerto Rican) or Asian. In contrast, blacks constituted only 8 percent of the teachers and less than 3 percent of the supervisors in the school system. This discrepancy was particularly evident in Ocean Hill-Brownsville, an extension of the Bedford-Stuyvesant "ghetto" that had previously been an area of Jewish residence.[22]

HAYOU's members believed that the self-destructive behavior among Blacks and other minorities in the form of drug use and violence were linked to the sense of inferiority and powerlessness produced by their colonial condition. In tackling the problem of inner-city unemployment, the HAYOU report recommended the creation of five local training and employment centers to facilitate and monitor remedial education, exploratory job training, and on-the-job training programs. To help them rebuild their self-esteem and self-worth, HAYOU proposed the creation of "arts and cultural affairs programs" to design and implement race-based "classes and workshops in the theatre, the dance, journalism and public relations, fashion and beauty culture, music, heritage, and film and sound techniques."[23] The art and culture programs were based on the theoretical assumption that the high school dropout rates of minority students, particularly Blacks and Puerto Ricans, reflected the kid's low self-esteem and frustration produced by their contact with the White middle-class value system of the school.

The efforts of HAYOU to peacefully solving the pressing problems in Harlem were hampered by the riots that followed the July 16, 1964, killing of James Powell, a Black youth who at the time of the incident was attending reading remedial classes in Harlem, by a white police officer. The Congress of Racial Equality (CORE) in Harlem and in the Bedford-Stuyvesant section of Brooklyn launched a series of manifestations and violent riots that extended from July 17 to July 22, resulting in 465 riot-related arrests. The race-based riots of the summer of 1964, made the HAYOU more politically attractive. However, the racial wound left by the 1964 riots and those that followed during the late 1960s, made it difficult, if not impossible for HAYOU to accomplish their main objective of rebuilding Black communities.[24]

The Kerner Commission, established by President Lyndon B. Johnson in 1967 to investigate the causes of the race riots, reported that these were the result of Black's frustrations and White discrimination. The Commission's recommendations included the creation of jobs, construction of new housing facilities, and an end to segregation. However, the Commission report was far from linking the riots to the ideology of internal colonialism. Instead, the report attributed the violence during the riots to the "unresponsiveness of local, white-dominated institutions to black demands for redress of grievances."[25] Conversely, lawyer and conflict resolution expert Richard E. Rubenstein suggested that

> blacks in revolt between 1964 and 1969 were obeying the anticolonial impulse familiar to students of the American Revolution and farmer uprisings, the Civil War and labor-management violence: they fought to rid their territory of the alien, to destroy his works, and to reclaim what they felt was rightly theirs.[26]

Robert Blauner, a sociologist, proposed a similar analysis in his book, *Racial Oppression in America*. According to Blauner, compared to Blacks and Native Americans, immigrants who voluntarily entered the United States (e.g., Cuban, Mexicans, Asians) experience racial discrimination differently.

> The crucial difference between the colonized Americans and the ethnic immigrant minorities is that the latter have always been able to operate fairly competitively within the relatively open spaces of the capitalist class order. They came voluntarily in search of a better life. . . . Finally, as white Europeans

they could achieve a sense of membership in the larger society by making minor modifications in their ethnic institutions.[27]

However, Blacks and Third World immigrants share the historical fact that they have been colonized and forced into a subordinate position in society by prejudiced Europeans for being "inherently alien, culturally degenerate, and biologically inferior."[28] Although the colonization analogy did not entirely fit the condition of Black-Americans due to historical and geographical differences between Black-Americans and Northern Africans, during the riots of the 1960s the ideology of internal colonization strengthen the individual and collective determination to resist oppression through any means necessary, including violence. And according to Blauner, it also boosted self-respect and self-esteem among Blacks.

> Despite the differences in objective conditions, violence seems to have served the same psychic function for young ghetto blacks in the 1960s as it did for the colonized of North Africa described by Fanon and Albert Memmi—the assertion of dignity and manhood.[29]

In the meantime, the push for integration led by members of the civil right movement found great resistance and mounting obstacles. This became evident in 1964 when a group of White and Black activists organized the Mississippi Freedom Democratic Party in 1964 in response to the reluctance of the Democratic Party to admit Black delegates in its National Convention. On June 17, 1966, at the Meredith Mississippi Freedom March, Black activist Stokely Carmichael expressed the frustration of many Blacks when he addressed the marchers and exhorted them to fight for Black Power. The following year, the publication of the *Black Power: The Politics of Liberation in America,* written by Stokely Carmichael and Charles V. Hamilton, outlined the anti-colonialist ideology that shaped the Black Power movement across the country. Carmichael and Hamilton recognized that language is a tool of domination: "The American educational system continues to reinforce the entrenched values of the society through the use of words."[30] The act of defining words and imposing those words and definitions is an exercise of power and oppression that must be confronted.

> "Integration" is . . . a current example of a word which has been defined according to the way white Americans see it. To many of them, it means black men wanting to marry white daughters; it means "race mixing"—implying bed and dance partners. To black people, it has meant a way to improve their lives—economically and politically. But the predominant white definition has stuck in the minds of too many people. . . . Black people must redefine themselves, and only *they* can do that. There is growing resentment of the word "Negro," for example,

because this term is the invention of our oppressor; it is *his* image of us that he describes. Many blacks are now calling themselves African-Americans, Afro-Americans, or black people because that is *our* image of ourselves.[31]

Although radical leaders welcomed Carmichael's separatist stand, integrationists rejected his "inflammatory" approach. Martin Luther King, Jr., called for an "end to the 'talk of black power.'" *The New York Times* quoted Dr. King as saying that Black people should ". . . never seek power exclusively for the Negro but the sharing of power with the white people . . . any other course is exchanging one form of tyranny for another. . . . Black supremacy would be as equally evil as white supremacy."[32] Similarly, John Lewis, former chairman of the Student Nonviolent Coordinating Committee, resigned from the organization in protest for the organization's new rhetoric of "black power;" a concept that he said, "threaten to alienate white friends of the rights movement."[33]

The Black Power movement defended and demanded the right of Blacks for self-determination and full political control of their communities and their institutions. In their view, these were necessary steps in the development of self-pride and progress among Blacks. The Black Muslims organization, a separatist organization established in the 1930s, embraced these goals and regained popularity and strength among many Blacks during the 1960s. They preached the inevitable destruction of the "white devils" and the dominance of Blacks, whose destiny was to create a separate nation within the United States.[34] Other Black organizations such as the Black Muslims Movement and the Black Panthers, advocated self-determination and were highly critical of the civil rights movement for failing in advancing the cause of Blacks in America. They were less willing to use the non-violence tactics advocated by Martin Luther King, Jr. and other civil rights leaders to destroy the Jim Crow system. However, what separated the Black Muslims Movement and the Black Panthers from Civil Rights organizations such as the NAACP was their separatist and nationalist agenda. With the financial support of Muslim leaders from around the world, particularly Muammar al-Qaddafi from Libya, the Black Muslims Movement accumulated about $70-million in small businesses and properties. Their political goal consisted of becoming independent from "any contact with whites." [35]

The numerous riots that took place in Black neighborhoods in Newark and Detroit during the Summer of 1967 made evident not just the level of frustration and anger that have been building up among Blacks but more importantly their capacity to organize and mobilize Black people. It also signified the dismissed of what Milton Gordon called the "draconian pressure-cooking assimilation" and the birth of what the National Advisory Commission on Civil Disorders described as "two societies, one black, one white—separate and unequal."[36] Almost a decade after the *Brown* decision, the level of trust among Blacks toward the mainstream institutions has dropped to significant levels. There was a perception that the federal government was not doing enough to reduce unemployment, segregation, and to stop the wave of lynching and racism facing Blacks and other minorities.[37] During her testimony in front of the National Advisory Commission on Civil Disorders in 1968, economist Vivian Henderson declared:

> No one can deny that all Negroes have benefited from civil rights laws and desegregation. . . . The fact is, however, that the masses of Negroes have not experienced tangible benefits in a significant way. This is so in education and housing. Expectations of Negro masses for equal job opportunity programs have fallen far short of fulfillment.[38]

NATIVE-AMERICAN AND LATINO RESISTANCE

Native Americans faced the challenge of preserving their well established identity and cultural heritage; a culture that was intrinsically linked to the land and its environment. It is not uncommon for scholars to portray Native Americans as helpless victims of European exploitation or as savages. However, Clara Sue Kidwell and Alan Velie indicate that this distortion obscures the complexity of the history of Native Americans.

> For centuries Indians were allies as well as enemies of whites in the Colonies and United States, and they gave as well as they got in battle. It is neither accurate historically nor fair to them to treat them as if they were nothing but hapless victims. Indians have much to be proud about in their history, and for whites to treat it is as an unmitigated series of disasters is dishonest as well as condescending.[39]

Paralleling Black and Latino militancy, during the 1960s Native Americans engaged in activism aimed at protecting their economic, political and cultural interests. On June 13, 1961, about one thousand American Indians representing more than one hundred tribes met at the University of Chicago for a week-long meeting to delineate a course of action against Congressional "termination" plan, and to call for the abolition of the Federal Bureau of Indian Affairs. the *New York Times* described the anti-termination feelings at the Chicago conference at follows:

> One word that inflames tribesmen now attending the American Indian Chicago Conference is "termination" . . . the Government recent policy of ending Federal trusteeship over the assets of tribes that are considered capable of handling

> their own money, property, services and affairs. Seven tribes have been "terminated" since the policy was enunciated in 1953. . . . The [Menominee'] assets, principally timberland and a sawmill, have been turned over to the Indians to be operated by a tribal corporation. . . . Mrs. Irene Mack, a member of the pre-termination advisory council, the administrative body of the tribe, said today the tribe's situation was a "chaotic mess." "It's steadily getting worse . . ." Taxation is not understood and is scaring the people to death. How are we going to get money to pay taxes?[40]

Anti-termination advocates also complained that Indians in terminated tribes are confronted with increasing unemployment and lack of medical and education services. This was the case with the Menominee Indians who were bribed to "approve" termination as a condition for the disbursement of money from the tribal funds.

That summer, some of the participants, particularly students, held a workshop in New Mexico that culminated with the formation of the National Youth Indian Council (NYIC). At their 1963 annual meeting the NYIC, led by Clyde Warrior, rejected activist Marlon Brandon's recommendation to join the civil right movement. Instead, the organization opted for engaging in locally-based activism aimed at protecting land and water rights.[41]

Meanwhile, the National Congress of American Indians (NCAI) strongly advocated for the improvement of the social and economic conditions of Indians. On January 20, 1964, an NCAI delegation met with President Johnson to discuss ideas on how to extend the President's "war on poverty" to the reservations; most of which had more than a fifty percent unemployment rate, and a school dropout rate of sixty percent. Among other things, the delegates requested "special consideration to Indians in the allocation of jobs, lower interest charges in federal loans, and protection against state policies aimed at gaining jurisdiction over Indian reservations.[42] It was the later concern, namely state jurisdiction over Indian affairs and properties as enacted under the termination act, that prompted the first "fish-in" protest that took place on March 2, 1964, in the Pacific Northwest, conducted by members of the NYIC, activist Marlon Brando, and other supporters. However, the precipitating factor was "the arrests of several Nisqually Indians for fishing off the reservation on Nisqually River, near Olympia, in what they insisted were the 'usual and accustomed' places for net fishing."[43] The "fish-in" served the purpose of calling public attention to the Indians' demand for federal protection against the violation of their rights under the treaty by the state governments.[44] Days later, on March 9, 1964, a group of Sioux Indians led by Allen Cottier, president of the San Francisco Bay branch of the American Indian Council, "took possession" of Alcatraz island under an 1868 treaty that gave the Sioux the right to claim Federal land not being used for a specific purpose. The invasion of the island, which lasted four hours, was "a protest against the 47 cents an acre awarded as a settlement by the Government for land taken from California Indians."[45] Although the protestors did not achieve the goals of assuming complete possession of the island and its transformation into a cultural center and an Indian university, the invasion demonstrated the organizational and activist capacity of Native Americans. Moreover, it reinforced the determination and the nationalist spirit of the Indians.

While members of the National Youth Indian Council emphasized the pressing needs of the Native Americans in rural communities, in 1968 the American Indian Movement (AIM) emerged as an activist organization to address the needs of Indians in urban America. The Indians who founded AIM first met in Minneapolis, Minnesota, in July 1968 to develop a political strategy to address the problems facing Indians in the Twin Cities area including police discrimination, unemployment, alcoholism, drug use, and violence. While across the country, Black and Latino had been rioting in demand for social change, in 1967, a Senate panel conducted a hearing to explain "why Indians do not riot."[46] In Senator Robert F. Kennedy's view, "some Negroes had grievances and . . . retaliate violently; Indians suffered in silence." In response, John Belindo, head of the National Congress of American Indians, argued that "demonstrations were not in the Indian character . . . It isn't their nature to demonstrate, . . . Indians have a deep reverence for the land; they wouldn't think of razing anything." Some of their demands, however, were not that different from the demands and concerns expressed by Blacks and Latinos through their riots: full control of the school system, the elimination of boarding schools, a curriculum that reflects and reinforces Indian values, educational television in rural areas, and bilingual education in the Head Start programs.[47] Like Black and Latino activists, Native American activism was also geared toward maintaining Indian pride and identity. As appendix C shows, Indian activism revolved around the issues of protecting their sovereignty, defining and expanding their legal rights, and the preservation of their cultural heritage.

For their part, Latinos showed great resistance to forced assimilation by embracing egalitarian pluralism. In the midst of a growing economy after World War II, the socioeconomic reality of Latinos was not very different from that of their Black counterparts, namely, high unemployment, violence, discrimination, segregation and deteriorating schools. The 1960 census showed that the median income of Latino males in California and Texas who have completed twelve years of schooling was 24 percent and 38 percent less than that of Anglos of equal educational standing.[48] For many Latinos, these findings challenged the commonly held middle-class assumption that more education improves income position. The census also showed that about 61 percent of Mexican-American males were concentrated in "low-skill manual occupations" compared to less than 28 percent of Anglos.[49]

In their fight for change, some Latino organizations combined electoral involvement with "the confrontation tactics used by Black militants in order to wrest concessions of economic and political power from the 'gringos.'"[50] The Viva Kennedy Movement was organized during the election period of 1960 to get Mexican-Americans involved in local and national politics. The movement, led by a group of successful middle class activists, believed the election of J. F. Kennedy for president was the best venue to address the needs and demands of the Latino people.[51] During the post-election period leaders and followers of the Viva Kennedy Movement had to face the fact that the Kennedy administration ignored its campaign promises. Moreover, four years later, President Johnson's war on poverty disappointed Latino voters who felt excluded from the planning process and from the national agenda.

> Planners and administrators of the new agencies were white liberals who were based in Washington. For the most part, they had never seen a Chicano and did not know his needs. These liberals, riddled with guilt feelings toward the Blacks and shaken by the urgency of the ghetto revolts, excluded the Chicano from the planning stages. Most of the money, jobs, and programs were directed to Blacks, even though in the Southwest the Chicano outnumbered the Black two or three to one. Many Chicano bureaucrats were committed at least to eroding "the Black-white syndrome" (the habit of white politicians and liberals of looking at problems through the perspective of the Black-white experience) that operated in the United States.[52]

Within the economic sector, Cesar Chavez led a massive unionization of migrant workers as a strategy to improve the working and living conditions of migrant workers across the country. In urban America, the Brown Berets, *La Raza Unida* and organized students like the Mexican American Youth Organization (MAYO) demanded political participation and the control of the education system. Equally important, in 1970 an organized group of Mexican Americans, known as *Católicos Por La Raza* (Catholics for the Race) protested in front of St. Basil's Church in Los Angeles demanding that the Catholic Church appointed more Mexican Americans within the decision making hierarchy of the Irish-controlled Church and that the Church join them in their "struggle to obtain self-determination."[53] In another protest in Mission, Texas, about a hundred Mexican-Americans "painted a statute of Our Lady of the Immaculate Conception brown."[54] For the protesters and their supporters, the act was an affirmation of their "browness" and an attempt at calling public attention to the economic conditions of Mexican-Americans; an issue that had been "a vague echo on the periphery of a hundred other considerations—black power, student power, Vietnam."[55] The student protest, particularly the 1968 protest in Los Angeles, highlighted the magnitude of the dissatisfaction and unity of Mexican Americans. They demanded a more active role of the federal and local governments in reducing the dropout rate of Latino students, eliminating school crowding, removal of racist teachers, and the hiring of more Chicano teachers and administrators. In terms of curriculum, the protestors claimed that "it was designed to obscure the Chicano's culture and to condition the students to be content with low-skilled jobs."[56]

The Latino protests produced short and long term results. In some cities, Anglo-dominated school boards capitulated and granted student's demands, and the Catholic Church was forced to become more actively involved in defending the interests of farm workers and students. The Mexican-American wave of protests during the 1960s forced the Johnson Administration to establish The Inter-Agency Committee on Mexican American Affairs in 1967, whose main goal was to find a solution to the Mexican American problems. One of the most celebrated victories of the Latino movement that came out of the committee hearings was the passage of the politically controversial Bilingual Education Act of 1968. Armed with scholarly research on bilingualism in education a group of experts persuaded the committee members about the need to implement bilingual education for Mexican Americans. The benefits of teaching Mexican American children in the native tongue range from increasing their self esteem to reducing their dropout rates. During her testimony, Hercella Toscano, a consultant for the San Antonio Language Research Project, declared:

> For the child of a non-English language background, systematic instruction in his mother tongue will enhance his self-image, it will enable him to experience greater success in conceptualizing and learning, it will increase his capacity to learn English as a second language and ultimately he will become bilingual.[57]

The act significantly impacted children and their families:

> By 1973 100,000 students were involved in 213 projects in 32 states and territories, and involving 19 languages other than English. Approximately 90% of these students were in Spanish/English programs, and most of these programs were Mexican-American programs.[58]

By the 1960s, the idea that educators should take into account the students' racial and ethnic background as they work with students was widely accepted by many academics and politicians. One of the most controversial legislative reforms of the 1960s was The Bilingual Education Act of 1968. As originally conceived, the act was aimed at helping Native Americans, and foreign born immigrants and their families in maintaining their language and culture. Opponents of bilingual education believed that teaching kids in their native tongue would hamper their assimilation into the mainstream society by reinforcing segregation. However, several studies conducted during the 1970s questioned the validity of this claim. The meta-analysis conducted by Rolf Kjolseth (1972), indicated that

> The great majority of bilingual programs (well over 80 percent) closely approximate the extreme of the assimilation model, while the remaining few are only moderately pluralistic. Thus, in direct contradiction to the usual program's statement of goals, the structure of "typical" programs can be expected to foster not the maintenance but rather the accelerated demise of the ethnic mother tongue. . . . The traditional policy of "Speak Only English" is amended to "We Will Speak Only English—just as soon as possible and even sooner and more completely if begin with a variety of the ethnic language rather than only English!"[59]

In explaining his finding, Kjolseth suggests that the lack of funding and the lack of trained personnel do not completely explain the failure of the bilingual and bicultural programs to promote pluralism. He agreed with previous researchers that many of these bilingual and bicultural programs have failed in achieving the pluralist goal because the schools remained alien to the values and needs of the ethnic communities and because they are bureaucratically run.[60] James Fallows' investigative report for the *Atlantic Monthly* supports the argument that bilingual education promotes assimilation. In his words,

> Before I traveled to some of the schools in which bilingual education was applied, I shared the skeptics' view. What good could come of a system that encouraged, to whatever degree, a language other than the national tongue? But after visiting elementary, junior high, and high schools in Miami, Houston, San Antonio, Austin, several parts of Los Angeles, and San Diego, I found little connection between the political debate over bilingual education and what was going on in these schools. . . . There is another fact about bilingual education, more difficult to prove but impressive to me, a hostile observer. Most of the children I saw were unmistakably learning to speak English. In the elementary schools, where the children have come straight out of all-Spanish environments, the background babble seems to be entirely in Spanish. The kindergarten and first- to third-grade classrooms I saw were festooned with the usual squares and circles cut from colored construction paper, plus posters featuring Big Bird and charts about the weather and the seasons. Most of the schools seemed to keep a rough balance between English and Spanish in the lettering around the room; the most Spanish environment I saw was in one school in East Los Angeles, where about a third of the signs were in English. . . . Bilingual education is inflammatory in large part because of what it symbolizes, not because of the nuts and bolts of its daily operation.[61]

NOTES

1. "Race Problem Seen in Indiana Capital: Increasing Frequency of Rows Between Negroes and Whites Raises Apprehensions." *The New York Times*, July 13, 1943, p. 42, BF section.

2. *The New York Times*, "Rumors Intensify Racial Problems" October 1, 1943, p. 36, BF section.

3. *Time* "Deep Trouble" June 28, 1943. http://www.time.com/time/printout/0,8816,790958,00.html# (accessed, October 31, 2008).

4. In *Shelley v. Kraemer*, the Supreme Court held "that in granting judicial enforcement of the restrictive agreements in these cases, the States have denied petitioners the equal protection of the laws and that, therefore, the action of the state courts cannot stand. We have noted that freedom from discrimination by the States in the enjoyment of property rights was among the basic objectives sought to be effectuated by the framers of the Fourteenth Amendment. That such discrimination has occurred in these cases is clear. Because of the race or color of these petitioners they have been denied rights of ownership or occupancy enjoyed as a matter of course by other citizens of different race or color." 334 U.S. 1 , 21. See entire case at: http://caselaw.lp.findlaw.com/scripts/getcase.pl?court=US&vol=334&invol=1.

5. See entire case at: http://caselaw.lp.findlaw.com/scripts/getcase.pl?court=US&vol=347&invol=483.

6. Civil Rights Act of 1957: Cabinet Paper—The Civil Rights Program—Letter and Statement by the Attorney General, April 10, 1956 https://eisenhower.archives.gov/research/online_documents/civil_rights_act/1956_04_01_Cabinet_Paper.pdf (accessed October 31, 2008).

7. David Delaney, *Race, Place, and the Law* (Texas: University of Texas Press 1998), p. 177.

8. *1952 Negro Year Book: A Review of Events Affecting Negro Life*, ed. Jessie Parkhurst Guzman (New York: Wm. H. Wise) 1952, p. 336–337.

9. Herbert Shapiro, *White Violence, Black Response* (Amherst: The University of Massachusetts Press, 1988), p. 351.

10. Franz Fanon, *The Wretched of the Earth* (New York: Grove Press, 1963), p.153.

11. Ibid., p. 153.

12. *The New York Times*, "Focus on Africa in New Quarterly: U.S. Negro Group Publishes Topical Journal Here." July 24, 1965, p. 18.

13. Benjamin Muse, *The American Negro Revolution*, (IN: Indiana University Press, 1968) p.182.

14. Gunnar Myrdal, *An American Dilemma: The Negro Problem and Modern Democracy* (New York: Harper and Row) 1944 [1962]. p. 1049. This comprehensive study was financed by the Carnegie Corporation through a $300,000 grant. The Corporation contracted Swedish scholar Karl Gunnar Myrdal to coordinate the effort of 75 experts to study the historical, economic, social and political conditions of Blacks in the United States. According to Paul Hanly Furfey, the Board of the Carnegie Corporation decided to contract Myrdal to avoid bias. The board "felt that desirable to

put in charge of the study a foreign scholars from some country "of high intellectual and scholarly standards but with no background or traditions of imperialism." (p. 65) (See, "Editorial Comment: Some Initial Observations on the Carnegie Corporation's Study of the Negro in America," *The Journal of Negro Education*, 1944, Vol. XII, No. 2, pp. 131–138; also "An American Dilemma: The Negro Problem and Modern Democracy" by Gunnar Myrdal, reviewed by Paul Hanly Furfey, *American Catholic Sociological Review*, 1944, Vol. 5, No. 1, pp. 65–67.

15. Ibid., p. 1050
16. Ibid., p. lxxi.
17. Ibid., p. 998.
18. Ibid., p. 1003.
19. Ibid., p. 1004.
20. Ibid., p. 1016.
21. Harlem Youth Opportunities Unlimited, Inc. *Youth in the Ghetto: A study of the consequences of powerlessness and a blueprint for change.* (New York: HARYOU), 1964, p. 78. HARYOU was founded in 1962 in Harlem by concerned citizens with the support of federal and state authorities. It was by Kenneth B. Clark, a black leader graduated from Columbia University with a PhD in psychology (after being denied admission at Cornell University due to his race). HARYOU was an alliance of public and private organizations interested in solving the social and economic problems facing the resident of Harlem who were mainly Blacks and Puerto Ricans. See, Gladys L. Knight, "Harlem Youth Opportunities Unlimited, HAYOU" in The *Encyclopedia of American Race Riots*, ed. Walter Rucker, James Nathaniel Upton. (CT: Greenwood Press), 2007, pp. 267–269.
22. Janet L. Abu-Lughod, *Race, Space, and Riots in Chicago, New York, and Los Angeles*. (NY: Oxford University Press) 2007, p. 183.
23. Harlem Youth Opportunities Unlimited, Inc., *Youth in the Ghetto*. p. 497.
24. See, Gladys L. Knight, "Harlem Youth Opportunities Unlimited, HAYOU," p. 269.
25. Richard E. Ruberstein, *Rebels in Eden* (MA: Little, Brown and Company) 1970, p. 147.
26. Ibid., p. 126.
27. Robert Blauner, *Racial Oppression in America*, (New York: Harper and Row) 1972, p. 85.
28. Ibid., p. 85.
29. Ibid., p. 91.
30. Stokely Carmichael and Charles Hamilton, *Black Power: The Politics of Liberation in America*. (New York: Random House) 1967, p. 37.
31. Ibid., p. 37.
32. *The New York Times*, "Dr. King Deplores 'Black Power' Bid: Supremacy by either race would be evil, he says." June 21, 1966, p. 30.
33. *The New York Times*, "Lewis Quits S.N.C.C.; Shuns Black Power." July 1, 1996, p. 1.
34. National Advisory Commission. *Report of the National Advisory Commission on Civil Disorders.*(Washington, DC: Government Printing Office, 1968), p. 229.

35. Paul Delaney, "Libya Said to Have Lent Black Muslims $3-Million," *New York Times*, February 2, 1973.

36. Milton M. Gordon, *Assimilation in American Life: The role of race, religion and national origins*. (New York: Oxford University Press) 1964, p. 106. National Advisory Commission. *Report of the National Advisory Commission on Civil Disorders*. (Washington, DC: Government Printing Office, 1968), p. 1.

37. See James Banks, "Multiethnic Education in the U.S.A.; Practices and Promises," in *Education in Multicultural Societies*, ed. Trevor Corner (New York: St. Martin Press, 1984).

38. National Advisory Commission. *Report of the National Advisory Commission on Civil Disorders*. (Washington, DC: Government Printing Office, 1968), p. 231.

39. Clara Sue Kidwell and Alan Velie, *Native American Studies* (Nebraska: University of Nebraska Press) 2005, p. 12.

40. *The New York Times*, "Indian Tribesmen Decry U.S. Policy: Oppose Federal Efforts to Terminate Trusteeship." June 15, 1961, p. 20.

41. Paul Chaat Smith and Robert Allen Warrior, *Like a Hurricane: The Indian Movement from Alcatraz to Wounded Knee*. (New York: The New Press), 1996, pp. 41–45.

42. *The New York Times*, "Johnson Pledges Help for Tribes" January 21, 1964, p. 15.

43. *The New York Times*, "Indian Map Protest in Washington State," March 1, 1964, p. 66.

44. See, Paul Chaat Smith and Robert Allen Warrior, *Like a Hurricane*, p. 45.

45. *Washington Post*, "Indian Tribe 'Captures' Alcatraz," March 10, 1964, p. A1 and A4.

46. *The New York Times*, "Senate Panel Hears Why the Indians Do Not Riot." December 16, 1967. p. 22.

47. Ibid., p.22.

48. Leo Gebler, Joan W. Moore and Ralph C. Guzman, *The Mexican-American People: The Nation's Second Largest Minority*. (London: Free Press) 1970, p. 196.

49. Ibid., 211.

50. *Washington Post*, "The Chicanos Want In" January 11, 1970, p. 29.

51. Ignacio M. Garcia, *Viva Kennedy Mexican Americans in Search of Camelot* (Texas: Texas A&M University Press) 2000.

52. Rodolfo Acuna, *Occupied America: The Chicano's Struggle Toward Liberation* (San Francisco: Canfield Press) 1972, p. 226.

53. *Washington Post*, "Prelate Target of Mexican-American Protests." January 5, 1970, p. 8.

54. Washington Post, "The Chicanos Want in." January 11, 1970, p. 29.

55. Ibid., p. 29.

56. Rodolfo Acuna, *Occupied America: The Chicano's Struggle Toward Liberation*, p.227.

57. U.S. Department of Health, Education, and Welfare, "The Mexican American: A New Focus on Opportunity, Testimony Presented at the Cabinet Committee Hear-

ings on Mexican American Affairs." El Paso, Texas, October 26–28, 1967. (Washington, DC: Government Printing Office) 1968.

58. Rolf Kjolseth, "Bilingual Education Programs in the United States: For Assimilation or Pluralism?" in *The Language Education of Minority Children*, ed. Bernard Spolsky (Rowley, MA: Newbury House Publishers, Inc., 1972), p. 2.

59. Ibid., p. 109.

60. Ibid., p. 110.

61. James Fallows, "Immigration: How it's affecting us," *The Atlantic Monthly*, November 1983, Vol. 252, No. 3. http://www.theatlantic.com/doc/198311/immigration (accessed December 10, 2008).

Chapter Three

Decolonizing Education: The Ethnic Studies Movement

During the 1960s and 1970s, the notion that ethnic and racial minorities have the right to maintain their language and cultural heritage was widely accepted and promoted. As a result, the ethnic studies model emerged as a pedagogical strategy to advance minority interests in education, and some would argue, achieving the American dream. The idea of teaching about the culture and language of specific ethnic groups in the United States dates back to colonial times and extends to the early part of the post-colonial era.

> Classes existed in the New England colonies, primarily to preserve German Lutheranism and German language and culture. In the latter decades of the eighteenth century, Japanese and Chinese schools were established in Hawaii and in California. In New York City, Jewish schools were established. These programs supplemented those of the public schools. Students attended ethnic schools in the evenings or on weekends.[1]

The revival of the ethnic studies model in the 1960s was due, in part, to the economic and political marginalization of ethnic minorities. As discussed in the previous chapter, during the 1960s and 1970s, Blacks, Native Americans, and Latinos developed a strong sense of ethnic pride that became translated into a nationalist and anti-colonialist spirit. The ethnic studies approach was conceived as a mechanism to understand and solve the pressing problems facing minorities as oppressed people through the decolonization of education. Ethnic studies advocates made the following assumptions: (1) each ethnic group is unique in terms of experiences within the larger society, (2) each group shows unique demographic patterns, and (3) minority groups are culturally homogenous as well as heterogeneous. It was further assumed that the worldviews of ethnic groups, as reflected in their literature, folklore, music, and art forms, must be included in the formal curriculum in order to provide a more accurate view of society.[2] Operating from those assumptions, ethnic studies proponents challenged the Eurocentric curriculum as reflected through its canon foundation. Hence, ethnic studies advocates demanded a more inclusive curriculum.[3]

As it turns out, during the 1960s, even the American Dream metaphor fell into question in light of the social and economic realities facing minority people. For instance, in 1967 the president of the National Congress of American Indians, John Belindo, told the U.S. senators that "the white man's school system, by trying to impose an alien culture on their children, was driving the children to alcoholism and suicide." What the Indian leaders wanted was "a voice in running the schools . . . and the schools to "teach Indian culture, not just a lot of unattainable middles class values." Mr. Belindo told the senators: "Indians couldn't care less about washing machines, about doves flying out of the kitchen windows, about other mainstream values. They wanted an education that enhanced their own cultural values"[4] Mr. Belindo's view was representative of the dissatisfaction with the establishment that prevailed among a large segment of the general population. From this perspective, education was defined as a "myth-maker" and a dehumanizing machine aimed at maintaining and promoting individualism, obedience, conformity, and consumerism, at the expense of group identity, creativity, and respect for the environment. Ethnic studies proponents demanded that curriculum developers take into account the ways in which the diverse background of minority groups have shaped their views and way of thinking and the ways through which the hidden curriculum reinforce existing practices of domination, discrimination, and inequality.

Politically, at the time minorities were pressing for self-determination, and autonomous control of their communities, desperate politicians called for immediate action to integrate ethnic and racial minorities within the social system. In 1969, referring to the situation of Blacks and Puerto Ricans in New York, Senator Jacob K. Javits told the media that "We're [in New York] running completely out of time. . . . One big mistake and it will be all over. It will be one big slum."[5] In the process of disentangling the dilemmas posed by insurgent minorities, system-oriented analysts created new labels to frame minority issues. During the late 1960s poverty, crime, and school drop outs were described as social problems facing the "underprivileged" as a result of years of "cultural deprivation." Within the political establishment, the notion of cultural deprivation meant that minority's deviation from the dominant culture, as evidenced by their reluctance to abandon their native cultural frame of reference, was the main cause of their social and economic disadvantage.[6] By the early 1970s, the cultural deprivation model had lost its appeal among academicians and educators. Critics persuasively argued that the academic and social disadvantage of minority members was a reflection of the failure of the education system to address the cultural and institutional needs of this growing segment of the population. It was assumed that a pluralistic system of education was needed to assist minorities and the poor in developing a sense of identity and cultural worth.[7] The argument was made that minority students had to labor ". . . with the handicap of a negative self-image. Clearly, if we are to upgrade achievement in these groups of individuals, the school must provide opportunities for experiences that modify negative attitudes toward the self."[8] The challenge for advocates of pluralism in education was how to turn theory into policy and practice.

THE ETHNIC HERITAGE STUDIES PROGRAM ACT OF 1972

Since the 1930s when Rachel D. DuBois founded the Bureau for Intercultural Education, most public schools and universities around the country had adopted some form of intercultural and ethnic studies program as part of their curriculum. To a great extent, the increasing body of literature on inter-ethnic relations facilitated the integration of intercultural pedagogies and practices in the classrooms. As mentioned earlier, the enforcement of the *Brown* decision made it evident that in most cases schools, teachers, students, parents, and staff where not ready or willing to change. In their efforts to comply with the desegregation mandate, education experts had to move fast and aggressively to at least show a good faith effort to desegregate and integrate minority students. In the process, school personnel faced the challenge of becoming intercultural in their pedagogy, the community demanded to be informed about what was going on inside the classrooms, and the schools demanded more resources to create an interracial environment.

In 1972, as the public and the media struggled to disentangle the facts of the Watergate Scandal and the events in Vietnam, the Nixon administration gave impetus to the intercultural agenda by signing the Ethnic Heritage Studies Programs Act (Title IX of the Elementary and Secondary Education Act of 1965). The original bill, introduced in Congress by Senator Richard S. Schweiker (Rep., PA), and by Representative Roman Pucinski (Dem., IL) was intended to make grants available to non-profit private organizations and public agencies and institutions for the development of ethnic studies program. After extensive congressional debates and hearings a compromise bill was passed on June 14, 1972, and on June 23, 1972, President Nixon signed the Ethnic Heritage Studies Act which authorized $15 million for fiscal 1973 to:

develop curriculum material for use in elementary and secondary schools and institutions of higher education relating to the history, geography, society, economy, literature, art, music, drama, language, and general culture of the group or groups with which the program is concerned and the contributions of that ethnic group or groups to the American heritage; Disseminate curriculum materials to permit their use in elementary and secondary schools and institutions of higher education throughout the Nation. Provide training for persons using or preparing to use, curriculum materials developed under the title. [To] cooperate with persons and organizations with a particular interest in the ethnic or group or groups with which the program is concerned to assist them in promoting, encouraging, developing, or producing programs or other activities which relate to the history, culture, or traditions of that ethnic group or groups.[9]

However, the legislators did not assign any appropriations for the bill until late 1973, when the House of Representative and the Senate reached the compromise of funding the Act but only for $2.5 million.[10] Despite the reduction in appropriation, the Ethnic Heritage Study Act generated significant public interest and community involvement. That year, the United States Office of Education, in charge of processing the requests for grants, received "1,026 proposals . . . in competition for 40 grants."[11]

In 1974, David E. Washburn conducted a survey of 715 school districts to investigate the presence and extent of the multi-ethnic studies programs in the country.[12] The final sample (397 participants) was predominantly composed of White students (between 91 percent and 100 percent), and teachers and administrators (91 percent to 100 percent). The study showed that of the 397 school districts responding the survey, 72.5 percent (288) reported having an ethnic studies curricula. Of the 288 schools reporting having ethnic studies curricula, 74 percent used "human relations training for teachers," and 70 percent used a "community involvement in school policy" in their attempt to promote cross-cultural understanding. Among those reporting not having an ethnic studies curricula, 48 percent and 39 percent offered "human relations training for teachers," and "community involvement in school policy," respectively. Of the 288 school districts with ethnic studies curricula, about 82 percent of them had been in operation for five years or less, and only 4.2 percent had been engaged in ethnic studies for ten years or more. Overall, the ethnic groups receiving the most significant attention in their ethnic curricula were Blacks, Mexican Americans, and Native Americans, with curricular inclusion rates of 92 percent, 71 percent, and 67 percent, respectively. An average of 25 percent of the ethnic studies curricula included the study of European Americans (Italians, German, English, French, Polish, and Russian). In terms of content, the ethnic studies curricula in the survey included topics such as history, social customs, culture, social structure, and personality.

THE COLLEGE ETHNIC STUDIES MOVEMENT

Although the Ethnic Heritage Act of 1972 was enacted in response to the need for interethnic respect and tolerance in schools, the act was also the product of the increasing activism of the ethnic-studies movements, particularly the Black studies movement, of the late 1960s. During that period, the notion of "ethnic studies" emerged as a radical solution for the cultural "decolonization" of minorities in the United States, and the eradication of exploitation. The argument was made that like colonized people in underdeveloped countries, minorities in the United States had been the victims of internal colonization; a condition that had destroyed their individual and collective identity and pride. As early as 1964, the HAYOU report had compared the conditions in Black neighborhoods to those found in colonial societies and recommended the implementation of study centers to address the academic and cultural needs of Black students.

> The goal of this program [Study Centers] will determine its content, namely, to teach the students how to read, write, spell, do arithmetic, and speak properly. These basic skills are essential for all other learning. Special incentives analogous to those motivating enthusiastic participation in athletics competition could be developed, e.g., playwriting contests, the winning plays to be published and produced by the Arts and Culture groups. An opportunity to relate educational accomplishments and racial identification would be provided by the use of material which emphasizes the overall civil rights struggle, the role of the Negro in American Culture, and the emergence of new nations in Africa and Asia.[13]

The proposal for the creation of art and culture groups in the Harlem area was based on the assumption that "the degree to which the student is able to identify in a positive manner with his history and his roots will in some way be related to an increase in the level of motivation to learn."[14] During the 1960s, minority leaders used this assumption to explain and justify the need for highly motivated and well-prepared teachers who can understand and teach minority students. It was also used to advocate for ethnically-based educational programs in schools and colleges.

The debate on the merits of ethnic studies programs during the 1960s centered not so much on the validity of the "ethnic motivation" assumption, but rather on the politics of education. For instance, in some colleges and universities, minority students identified themselves as "Third World" students who had a common political cause with the national and international working class. This tactic was aimed at creating political alliances between national and international forces of decolonization, and to dramatize the deplorable conditions of minority groups in the United States. As part of their agenda, minority students and civic leaders demanded the creation of "ethnic studies" programs, to be led by minorities, as a vehicle to correct the intellectual biases of the established Eurocentric and colonialist curriculum. Politically, it was a demand for the restructuration power relationships within academia, and eventually in society.

The ethnic studies model was a radical response against the conservatism of the ethnic "area studies" model; which were allegedly sponsored by the CIA and private organizations, such as the Ford Foundation, The Rockefeller Foundation, and the Owens-Corning Fiberglass Corporation to protect and promote American geo-political and military interests in Africa, Asia, and Latin America.

> The initial objective was primarily cultural, but as the international crisis developed in the late 1930s, the programs which The Rockefeller Foundation had sponsored became important assets in the development of language and area training for the Armed Forces. Since the War, with the United States catapulted into world leadership, it has been necessary to pursue simultaneously the dual objectives of cultural enrichment and the strengthening of national capacities for sound foreign policy.[15]

The radicalism and strength of the ethnic studies movement became evident in San Francisco State College in 1968. For years, the leadership of the Black Student Union had criticized the university curriculum for its pro-Western, White bias; a criticism that was commonly voiced by minority students across the country. In 1966, the Black Student Union obtained a victory when the university administration created the Black Arts and Cultures Series and a year later, the Black studies programs. John H. Bunzel describes the birth of the program as follows:

> The Black Arts and Culture Series was instituted in the fall semester (1966) as a part of the Experimental College. The purpose was to introduce a positive focus on the life experiences of black people in America. Classes covered the areas of history, law, psychology, humanities, social science, and dance. One year later, the first Black Studies was enacted, with a total of eleven classes for which thirty-three units of college credit were given. Several hundred students, black and white, enrolled in the courses, which were taught on a voluntary or part-time basis either by members of the faculty or graduate students sympathetic to the program.[16]

Although Nathan Hare, the first coordinator of the Black studies program at San Francisco State College, recognized the merits of the program, he had a more ambitious and revolutionary plan: to establish an autonomous department of Black studies exclusively for Black faculty and Black students. In his view,

"It may be necessary eventually to distinguish Black education for Blacks and Black education for whites." White teachers do not understand and cannot teach black history, therefore, "Black people must declare void what the white slave master has written and must begin to write their own history and direct their destiny."[17] What made his plan for a Black studies program different from other ethnic studies programs was its mandatory field work whereby Black students were required to engage in work to transform Black neighborhoods. Hare's formal proposal went through extensive review by university administrators and the Black Students Union. Questions aroused, particularly among those opposed to Hare's plan, as to whether white teachers would be hired, whether the program would admit white students and the possibility of integrating Blacks studies within the existing academic programs rather than having a separate program on the Black experience. Hare's position was clear: the programs were for Black students only. Also controversial was the demand by the Black Student Union that all "Black Studies courses being taught through various other departments immediately become part of the Black Studies Department. . . ." and that the Department's chair, faculty, and staff "have the sole power to hire faculty and to determine the destiny of its department."[18] After seventy-three days of student-led protests, in 1969 the university established the College of Ethnic Studies at San Francisco State College. That year, a student-led strike at the University of California Berkeley led to the creation of a Department of Ethnic Studies. From their conception, both programs focused "on the histories, literatures, and politics of Asian Americans, Chicanos/Latinos, Native American Indians, and African Americans," as they relate to the analysis of "structural forms of oppression and . . . the intersections of race, ethnicity, and other forms of identity and social status."[19]

At Hunter College in New York, in 1969 the faculty and the administration voted in favor of a resolution to establish a department to offer courses leading to "a major concentration in both black and Puerto Rican studies."[20] Following the college's decision, a group of white students demanded the establishment of a department of Jewish studies. At Harvard, on April 10, 1968, six days after the assassination of Martin Luther King, Jr., the Association for African and Afro-American Students published an advertisement in the Harvard Crimson demanding "the establishment of an endowed chair for a Black Professor, creation of courses relevant to Black students, more Black faculty members, and the admission of more Black students proportionate to their percentage of the population as a whole." In response, the Harvard administration created the Standing Committee on Afro-American Studies to develop a plan to create an Afro-American studies program. In 1969, after months of tense deliberations and planning the committee appointed nine faculty members to teach Afro-American courses, created seven new courses, and announced a proposal to establish the W. E. B. Du Bois Institute for Afro-American Research; which was founded in 1975.[21] At Ohio State University, in 1968 members of the black Student Union "took over the administration building and held top university officials under restraint for hours while presenting a list of grievances involving alleged racial prejudice." The continuing pressure of the Black Union led to the establishment of Black Studies division in 1969, and in 1972 it became a department.[22] Boston University, Notre Dame, Duke University, North Carolina College, North Carolina A&T, University of Michigan, and the University of Wisconsin also faced protests or threats of protests by organized ethnic minorities. At these and other campuses, the administrators claimed that they had developed a "master plan for handling confrontation" produced by ethnic minorities and anti-Vietnam war protestors.[23] However, a study conducted by the Urban Research Corporation revealed that racially based protests accounted for about 49 percent of the approximately 89 protests that took place in 1969, and the rest were war-related.[24]

THE ETHNIC STUDIES MOVEMENTS IN COMMUNITY COLLEGES

Community colleges were not immune to the ethnic riots taking place in four-year colleges and universities across the country. Under the direct or indirect influence of Black student organizations, Black students at some community colleges produced "position" papers regarding issues and demands affecting non-white students on college campuses. John Lombardi, who has done extensive research on the ethnic studies movement in community colleges, describes the general format of the position papers as follows:

> The general tenor of the papers was the same, whether prepared in Cleveland, Los Angeles, Chicago, San Jose, or Seattle. (1) An introductory statement on the activities of the organization during the recent past and the "new attitude . . . within the black student bodies, on the sufferings of the black man under a society that fosters racism," and a determination to alter the picture for America's benefit as well as our own. . . ." (2) A list of numbered demands, (3) A request for a meeting with the president "to discuss acceptance of these demands . . ., (4) A time limit or ultimatum, (5) A threat or warning about the consequences of failure to respond satisfactorily.[25]

It was not uncommon for the administrators to issue their own public response to the students' demands in which they specified that the term "demand" was unacceptable to the administration and that they would prefer to call them "requests," and that the students' leadership should "schedule" an appointment to discuss the "requests." Given the organizational structure and relatively small size of community colleges, the student demands were normally addressed to the president of the institution, many of whom responded with "statements of understanding and sympathy, and a desire to help the black students."[26] To a great extent, the list of demands was not that different from the demands in four-year institutions. It included the creation of Black studies programs, remedial and freshman orientation courses, employment for blacks, and removal of discriminatory practices in enrollment. The official response to the students' demands ranged from promising to "redress the grievances that had led to campus disturbances" to complete "refusal to accede to any of the demands." With few exceptions, the overall approach taken by community college presidents was an "extraordinarily careful and respectful attention" to the demands as a way of preventing violent race riots.[27]

THE GROWTH OF ETHNIC STUDIES PROGRAMS

For some politicians and scholars, the increasing demand for ethnic studies programs was not just a threat to the traditional academic curriculum but also an "excuse to practice racism in reverse, that is, separate facilities for Black students."[28] The suspicion that ethnic studies programs were segregationist and propagandistic became evident in 1969 when the Federal government informed the Antioch College (and all colleges) that they "will lose Federal funds if it continues to operate a segregated black studies program."[29] The prominent scholar and former director of the HAYOU project, Kenneth Clark assumed a similar position and resigned from his post at the Antioch College's board of trustees in protest against whites being kept out of the Black school's Afro-American Studies Institute. In an interview for the *New York Times* in 1973, he described black studies programs as a "hoax."

> I think they're a hoax. I think is an indication that white educational decision makers don't really take their responsibility to black students seriously. If they did, they would not perpetrate this hoax. It's an easy way out. It's an easy way of dealing with an emotional problem. If you contrast the method of setting up black studies with the methods of setting up a serious thing such as nuclear physics or serious courses in the humanities, you will see that black studies have just become the colored section, the Jim Crow section. They reflect segregated academia, which is to me intolerable. Now, having said that, I will also say that there have been significant deficiencies in the teaching of American history, politics, economics. You know, the academic world has been infected by racism, too. The cure, though, does not seem to me to lie in isolation of black studies. The cure is much more complex than that . . . You have to develop scholarship

in history, in literature, in the humanities which reflects the racial truths of America rather than racial myths. Now that's a hell of a lot more difficult than black studies programs. The emptiness and the racism inherent in black studies will make that even more difficult.[30]

Despite the opposition, it has been estimated that by 1972, "about 200 institutions [had] some sort of black studies program, and that another 400 [offered] courses in black history or culture."[31] The proliferation of Black studies programs was the product of student pressure and administrators, politicians, and private organizations who were "sympathetic to" or "afraid of" student activism and their demands. By the early 1970s, many states had mandated the incorporation of "ethnic studies" components in colleges and university programs, whereas in other states institutions of higher education voluntarily or under minority pressure incorporated ethnic studies components into their programs. In dealing with the financial constrains facing colleges and universities, many of them solicited the assistance of philanthropic organizations, particularly the Ford Foundation.

The involvement of the Ford Foundation in the development of Black studies programs in the United States has been well documented.[32] It has been estimated that between 1950 and 1971 the Ford Foundation awarded "more than $250 million" to colleges and organizations dedicated to advancing educational opportunities for Black students.[33] In 1969, the Foundation approved $891,800 for Black-studies activities, and $883,533 to support seven Black studies programs (appendix D). By 1971, the Ford Foundation had approved twenty Black studies grants specifically intended to incorporate Black-related topics into various disciplines, and for academic activities related to Black studies. Appendix E illustrates the magnitude of the involvement of the Ford Foundation in the development of Black studies in some of the most prestigious universities in the country. However, a survey conducted by the United States Office of Education in 1974 showed that for the most part Black Studies programs were financed through the institutional budget, and they operated as autonomous units. Of the twenty-nine programs included in the survey, twenty-two were financed by the institution, three were underwritten by grants from private foundations, and four were federally funded. Overall, in the majority of these programs the faculty was without academic rank or tenure, and those in tenure rank mainly held joint appointments in Black studies and other departments from which they obtained tenure.[34]

In her book, *White Money, Black Power*, Noliwe M. Rooks attributes the Ford Foundation's involvement in the development of Black studies programs to the influence of McGeorge Bundy, who was the Foundation's president from 1966 to 1979.

One event functions as ground zero for the Ford Foundation's commitment to initiating Black Studies as a step toward finally and fully addressing the "Negro Problem" in America. The beginning of the public association between the Foundation and African American Studies came at the behest of Bundy in 1968. That year, in a speech at Yale University, the former dean of Harvard University began to shape the feel, focus, and future of African American Studies as it entered the academic universe. The topic of the conference was Black Studies, and those who participated were called together to support the position of that university's Black Student Alliance, in its call for "including the study of Afro-American societies and cultures in the curriculum of Yale College."[35]

According to Rooks, "The strategy crafted by McGeorge Bundy and the Ford Foundation appealed to campus administrators, who believed it offered a solution to the problems of campus unrest, and to years of ignoring African American communities."[36] As Rooks implicitly recognizes, the strategy was limited to providing grant money for reforming the existing curriculums rather than for creating "autonomous and separate" Black studies departments. This means that the Ford Foundation was not amenable to help in achieving the main goal of the Black studies movement in most college campuses, namely, making ethnic studies a legitimate academic and intellectual field of study.

Fabio Rojas's analysis in *From Black Power to Black Studies* provides a more accurate interpretation of the involvement of the Ford Foundation in the development of Black studies programs.

> The decoupling of protest from soliciting and acquiring funds suggests that protest has an indirect effect on philanthropic organizations and their clients. In some cases, philanthropists will try to directly influence movement groups, the process studied by nonprofit scholars. In other cases, such as the Ford Foundation's support of black studies, protest sets institutional agendas and defines interests but does not affect decisions regarding new practices. A nonprofit group's intervention may be a response to a protest, but resources are awarded according to the conventions of the nonprofit sector and the targeted institutional domain.[37]

Consistent with Roja's interpretation, it also is possible to argue that the Foundation's financial support for Black studies programs was part of the organization's philanthropic mission including "reducing racial tensions."[38] Appendix F contains a list of the minority-oriented grant activities of the Foundation from 1968 to 1969. Overall, the data suggest that the Foundation founded programs and activities that were geared toward expanding job opportunities, education, and political participation for minority groups. The Foundation's commitment with the civil rights movement is also reflected in their support for human relations, legal defense, and law education organizations such as the N.A.A.C.P., and the Southwest Council of La Raza, "the largest national Hispanic civil rights and advocacy organization in the U.S."[39]

The civil rights movement and the Black studies movement of the late 1960s created the conditions for other ethnic groups to demand equality in education. Between 1964 and 1974, the Ford Foundation has approved $3,452,488 for Mexican American, Puerto Rican, and Native American studies (see appendix G). By the late 1970s, ethnic studies programs were well established across the country; about 760 ethnic studies programs had been in operation for approximately six years. Jewish American and Slavic American studies programs were two of the oldest programs in existence by 1978, 10.7 years, and 7.5 years respectively (appendix H).[40]

OPPOSITION TO ETHNIC STUDIES PROGRAMS

Perhaps the most common criticism against ethnic studies programs was expressed by Kenneth Clark when he defined ethnic studies programs as the "Jim Crow section" of academia, and as an easy way out of the "minority problem" on White-dominated campuses.[41] Harry Morgan, dean of the Black Studies Institute at Ohio University, expressed a similar concern during an interview for the *Chronicle of Higher Education* in 1972. According to the report, Mr. Morgan was concerned "that black studies centers may become a kind of black ghetto on white campuses. He notes that when the curriculum vitae of a black scholar is received on campus, it invariably is sent to him, "regardless of the person's academic discipline." The interview of Black students and college personnel in the early 1970s revealed a series of equally important criticisms against ethnic studies programs. Black students criticized the ethnic studies programs for "being too academic or irrelevant to the needs of the black community" and for serving to "pacify" black students. There was an overall agreement among the interviewees that the programs were not only inadequately funded, but also understaffed, and poorly implemented. Compounding the problem, many ethnic studies advocates openly claimed that ethnic studies programs should be administered, taught and attended by minorities only. It was assumed that Whites were not qualified to understand and to teach about the minority experience.[42] The opinion of John Hope Franklin, a history professor at the University of Chicago, reflected the overall feeling among critics of ethnic studies programs:

> Overnight, they [administrators] established courses and placed them in the hands of persons whose greatest talent seems to be in wringing their hands and

desperately trying to find out something about the history of Negro Americans before the beginning of the next meeting of the class. Ignorance abounds not only among would-be white teachers of black history but also among would-be black teachers of black history. The tragic fact is that there are not sufficient competent teachers to meet the demands.[43]

Some opponents of ethnic studies programs portrayed them as intellectually inferior "affirmative action" programs populated by unqualified or under-qualified "nationalist" and "segregationist" activists.[44] The perceptual link between ethnic studies and affirmative action has been interpreted as a byproduct of minority students' demand for minority faculty and staff as part of their negotiations during their riots.

Typically, advocates of black studies who called for drastic curriculum changes, particularly in the social sciences and humanities, simultaneously pressed for changes in faculty hiring procedures. Specifically, they wanted to insure that teachers in all of the new, and in some of the old, courses would be drawn from the ranks of blacks, even though they might not display the customary qualifications. Similarly, Chicano, Puerto Rican, and some Native American and Asian students subsequently insisted that members of their own groups be hired to teach courses and administer programs that they had been able to impose upon a reluctant and frequently hostile academic establishment.[45]

Forty years after the establishment of the first Black studies department in San Francisco College, this view of ethnic studies programs persists, as professor Mark Goldblatt's words clearly illustrate:

But the epistemological nadir of any university is found in the wacky world of ethnic and gender studies: black studies, Africana studies, Chicano studies, Latino studies, Puerto Rican studies, Middle Eastern studies, Native American studies, women's studies, gay and lesbian studies, et al. The suggestion that "studying" is involved in any of these subjects is laughable; they are quasi-religious advocacy groups whose curricula run the gamut from historical wish fulfillment (the ancient Egyptians were black; the U.S. Constitution was derived from the Iroquois Nation) to political axe grinding (the Israelis are committing genocide against the Palestinians; the U.S. is committing genocide against the people of Cuba) to gynocentric self-help (reasoning from verifiable data is a tool of male domination, to which the experiential impressions of women are a necessary antidote) to circumstantial special pleading (Lincoln was gay because, well, he was a nice guy; Hitler, not so nice, therefore not gay). Contesting the status quo is the raison d'etre of these departments. No idea is beyond the pale — except, of course, the suggestion that the status quo might somehow be valid.[46]

There also was a concern that Blacks ethnic studies programs, which were highly concentrated in the social sciences and education programs, would seduce minority students away from more "serious and academically demanding areas of study."[47] In an interview for *The New York Times* in 1971, Robert Jackson, a Black student at Cornell, complained that "at this point, black students should be concentrating on the physical and biological sciences. . . . We need more people in agriculture, oceanography, nutrition, and medicine."[48] As it turned out, the issue was more complex. In 1982, a major study sponsored by the Higher Education Research Institute and the Ford Foundation found that ". . . virtually all four of the minority groups under consideration [Blacks, Chicanos, Puerto Ricans, and American Indians] avoid the biological sciences, engineering, and the physical sciences and mathematics" and they show a predilection for the social sciences and education.[49] The study attributed this pattern of academic preferences to the "relatively low levels of academic preparation among all minority groups at the precollegiate level."[50] This interpretation is consistent with the finding of another major study conducted by Sanford Dornbusch which blames the schools' tracking systems for the underrepresentation of minorities in "college-prep math and science courses." The study found, that "the proportion of high-ability African-American and Latino American students not taking college prep courses in math and science was more than twice that of white and Asian American students of the same ability level."[51] It was believed that once in college, many ill-prepared minority students become attracted to academic areas which have a strong emphasis on ethnicity, and for which they feel qualified to succeed. However, according to the *Journal of Blacks in Higher Education*, Black studies has been "a very unpopular major for black students nationwide."[52] For many years, ethnic studies and related fields ranked among the lowest in preference among all ethnic groups, whereas business management ranked first in preference particularly among Blacks. However, ethnic studies programs have attracted a significant number of white students since almost 56 percent of the bachelor's degrees in ethnic studies-related areas were granted to White students. Hence, the idea that ethnic studies are for ethnic minorities is not completely supported by the statistics. It is possible that even in universities with a large White population of students the entire campus benefits from the ethnic studies courses offered regardless of the number of those majoring in ethnic studies programs. As Stanlie M. James, chair of the Department of Afro-American Studies at the University of Wisconsin at Madison puts it, "here at Wisconsin most of our students are European-Americans, as is nearly half of our faculty. This faculty is committed to African-American scholarship and teaching that is relevant to all students, regardless of color or nationality . . ."[53] Equally relevant is Robert S. Boynton's commentary in his article "The New Intellectuals" to the effect that ethnic studies programs have evolved from the old "identity, victimization, and alienation" paradigms to a new paradigm under which race and ethnicity are perceived as "manifestation of a larger American project; it conceives of the problems of African Americans [and other minority groups] as inseparable from the problems of America." The list of the new intellectuals transforming the field of ethnic studies includes Toni Morrison, Shelby Steele, Henry Louis Gates, Jr., and Cornel West; a group of intellectuals for whom "blackness is not a material object, an absolute, or an event, "but only a 'trope.'" The message coming from these "new intellectuals," particularly Cornel West, is clear: "we need a new paradigm that starts with "a frank acknowledgement of the basic humanness and Americanness of each of us,". . . . "if we go down, we go down together."[54]

NOTES

1. Prentice H. Baptiste, *Multicultural Teacher Education: Preparing Educators to Provide Educational Equity*, (Washington, DC: American Association of Colleges for Teacher), 1980, p. 116.

2. Ibid., 119.

3. Patricia Zavella, "Living on the Edge: Everyday Lives of Poor Chicano/Mexicano Families," in *Mapping Multiculturalism*, ed. Avery F. Gordon and Christopher Newfield (Minneapolis: University of Minnesota Press), 1996, pp. 362–386.

4. Laura Ross, *Inventing the Savage: The Social Construction of Native American Criminality*, (Austin: University of Texas Press), 1998, pp. 65–66. Also, "Civil Rights." *The San Francisco Examiner*, San Francisco California, Sunday, December 24, 1967, pp. 80–81. https://www.newspapers.com/image/458599144 (accessed November 4, 2008).

5. "The Changing City: Social Tensions," *The New York Times*, June 7, 1969, p.1.

6. Thomas C. Hoog and Marlin R. McComb, "Cultural Pluralism: Its Implications for Education," *Education Leadership*. December 1969, Vol. 27, No. 3, pp. 235–238.

7. B. C. VanKoughnett and Merle E. Smith, "Enhancing the Self-Concept in School," *Education Leadership*. December 1969, Vol. 27, No. 3, pp. 253–255. See also, John A. Ether, "Cultural Pluralism and Self-Identity." *Education Leadership*. December 1969, Vol. 27, No. 3, pp. 232–234.

8. VanKoughnett and Smith, "Enhancing the Self-Concept in School," p. 253.

9. Donald G. Hohl and Michael G. Wenk, "The Rodino's Bill and the Ethnic Heritage Studies Act," *International Migration Review*, Summer, 1973, Vol. 7, No. 2, pp. 191–194.

10. James M. Anderson, "The Evolution and Probable Future of Ethnic Heritage Studies," (College Park, MD: ERIC Document Reproduction Service) 1979, ED 184964. During a conversation with a House representative, James M. Anderson

was told that the trust of the congressional session considering the Heritage Studies Act was to "disapprove any requests for new appropriations." See also, Zake, Ieva. "Nixon vs. the G.O.P: Republican Ethnic Politics, 1968-1972." *Polish American Studies* 67, no. 2 (2010): 53–74. http://www.jstor.org/stable/41162460.

11. Ibid., p. 12.

12. David E. Washburn, "Multicultural Education Programs, Ethnic Studies Curricula, and Ethnic Studies Materials in the United States Public Schools." (College Park, MD: ERIC Document Reproduction Service) 1974, ED 180944.

13. Harlem Youth Opportunities Unlimited, Inc., *Youth in the Ghetto*, pp. 419–420.

14. Ibid., p. 416.

15. Charles B. Fahs, "A Reexamination of Rockefeller Foundation Program in Area Studies." Memorandum to the Rockefeller Board of Trustees, 1954. https://rockfound.rockarch.org/documents/20181/35639/A+reexamination+of+Rockefeller+Foundation+program+in+area+studies+PDF.pdf/902c2b68-25f3-4a1b-82f5-5adaa7996ca0. (accessed November 4, 2008). See also, Robert Witanek, "Students, Scholars, and Spies: The CIA on Campus" *Covert Action Information Bulletin*, Winter 1989, pp. 25-28. http://www.cia-on-campus.org/witanek.html (accessed November 4, 2008). See also, Ellen M. Gumperz, "Foreign Area Studies In American Higher Education" Interim Report, U.S. Department Of Health, Education, And Welfare, September 1966. https://ia801303.us.archive.org/14/items/ERIC_ED010604/ERIC_ED010604.pdf (accessed November 4, 2008).

16. John H. Bunzel, "Black Studies at San Francisco State," in *Confrontation: The Student Rebellion and the Universities*, ed. Daniel Bell and Irving Kristol (New York: Basic Books) 1969, p. 27.

17. Ibid., p. 28.

18. Ibid., pp.42–34.

19. See, http://ethnicstudies.berkeley.edu/; http://www.sfsu.edu/~ethnicst/home3.html (accessed November 3, 2008).

20. "Hunter to Offer Black and Puerto Rican Studies: White Student Group Urges Faculty to Set Up Jewish Program in the Fall, Too." *The New York Times*, February 27, 1969, p. 25.

21. University of Harvard's "Department of African and African American Studies Website" http://aaas.fas.harvard.edu/about_the_department/chronology.html (accessed November 13, 2008). See also, *The New York Times*, "Black Studies Come of Age," April 30, 1980, p. SM12. In this article, Professor Henry Rosovsky is quoted as describing the meetings that led to the Black Studies program as "an academic Munich."

22. "Indictment Name 34 at Ohio State University in Student Protest," *The New York Times*, June 1, 1968, p. 22. See also, http://aaas.osu.edu/ (accessed November 13, 2008).

23. "Students Shifting Tactics in Nation," *The New York Times*, September 14, 1969, p. 1.

24. "Campus Protests Reported on Rise: Rate of Eruption Placed at One a Day in 2-year Study," *The New York Times*, March 29, 1970, p. 72.

25. John Lombardi, "The Position Papers of Black Student Activists." (College Park, MD: ERIC Document Reproduction Service) 1970, ED 042453.

26. John Lombardi, "The President's Reaction to Black Student Activism." (College Park, MD: ERIC Document Reproduction Service) 1970, ED046390).

27. Ibid., p. 13.

28. Sam Bluefarb, "Ethnic Studies: A Counter-Proposal," *The Bulletin of the Rocky Mountain Modern Language Association.* June 1971, Vol. 25, No. 2, pp. 65.

29. "U.S. Warns Antioch on Black Studies," *The New York Times*, March 6, 1969, p. 26.

30. "Kenneth Clark's Revolutionary: Just Teach Them to Read., *The New York Times*, March 18, 1973, p. SM256.

31. John A. Crowl, "Black Studies: The Bitterness and Hostility Lessen, but Criticism Persists." *Chronicle of Higher Education*, 1972, Vol. 6, No. 34, p. 6.

32. Noliwe M. Rooks, *White Money, Black Power: The Surprising History of African American Studies and the Crisis of Race in Higher Education*, (Boston: Beacon Press), 2006, pp. 106–108. Fabio Rojas, *From Black Power to Black Studies: How A Radical Social Movement Became an Academic Discipline.* (Baltimore, MD: John Hopkins University Press) 2007. Ford Foundation, *Inclusive Scholarship: Developing Black Studies in the United States. A 25th Anniversary Retrospective of Ford Foundation Grant Making, 1982–2007.* (New York: Ford Foundation) 2007.

33. Rooks, *White Money, Black Power,* pp.106–108.

34. Elias Blake Jr. and Henry Cobb, *Black Studies: Issues in Their Institutional Survival*, (Washington, DC: US Department of Health, Education, and Welfare). 1976, pp. 4–5.

35. Rooks, *White Money, Black Power*, p. 75.

36. Rooks, *White Money, Black Power*, p. 59.

37. Fabio Rojas, *From Black Power to Black Studies,* pp. 165–166.

38. Ibid., p. 137.

39. See, http://www.nclr.org/content/viewpoints/detail/42500/ (accessed December 10, 2008). Also, https://oac.cdlib.org/findaid/ark:/13030/tf858006dc/ (accessed January 24, 2019).

40. David E. Washburn, *Ethnic Studies in the United States: Higher Education.* Washington, DC: ERIC, 1981, (ED 206 232).

41. John A. Crowl, "Black Studies," p. 7.

42. "The Dilemma of Black Studies, *Time*," Friday May 02, 1969. http://www.time.com/time/magazine/article/0,9171,900814,00.html (accessed December 1, 2008). See also, Clemmon E. Vontress, "Black Studies-Boon or Bane," *Journal of Negro Education*, Vol. 39, No. 3, Summer 1970, pp. 192–201.

43. John A. Crowl, "Black Studies," p. 7. See also, *Time*, "Teaching Black Culture," Friday June 14, 1968. http://www.time.com/time/printout/0,8816,900132,00.html (accessed December 3, 2008).

44. Noliwe M. Rooks, *White Money, Black Money,* p. 125. See also, Vontress, "Black Studies," p. 194.

45. Jane Cassels Record and Wilson Record, "Ethnic Studies and Affirmative Action: Ideological Roots and Implications for the Quality of American Life," *Social Science Quarterly*, September 1974, Vol. 55, No. 2, p. 503.

46. Mark W. Goldblatt, "W. Churchill." *National Review*, February 9, 2005.

47. "Kenneth Clark's Revolutionary: Just Teach Them to Read," *The New York Times*, p. 261.

48. "African Studies Center at Cornell Develops Practical and Scholarly Skills," *The New York Times*, January 5, 1971, p. 39.

49. Alexander W. Astin, Helen S. Astin, Kenneth C. Green, Laura Kent, Patricia McNamara, and Melanie Reeves Williams, *Minorities in American Higher Education: Recent Trends, Current Prospects, and Recommendations.* (California: Jossey-Bass, Inc.), 1982, p. 68.

50. "Kenneth Clark's Revolutionary: Just Teach Them to Read," p. 261.

51. "School Tracking Harms Millions, Sociologist Finds," *Stanford News Service*, March 3, 1994. News Release, Stanford University News Service. http://news-service.stanford.edu/pr/94/940302Arc4396.html (accessed November 20, 2008).

52. "Black Studies is an Unpopular Major," *The Journal of Blacks in Higher Education*, No. 36, Summer 2002, pp. 14–15. http://www.jstor.org/stable/3133905 (accessed December 2, 2008).

53. "The Present and Future of Black Studies," *Letters to the Editor*," Stanlie M. James, Chair, Department of Afro-American Studies, University of Wisconsin, Madison, *Chronicle of Higher Education*, May 27, 2005.

54. Robert S. Boynton, "The New Intellectuals," *The Atlantic Monthly*, March 1995, p. 66.

Chapter Four

The Birth of Multiculturalism

As shown in the previous chapter, in general, ethnic studies programs are designed around a single ethnic or racial group whose demands have forced university administrators to create autonomous or semi-autonomous ethnic studies departments or schools. Many of these departments will grant undergraduate or graduate majors or minors in their respective specialization. By contrast, multiculturalism represents an ideology that stresses the importance of introducing ethnic and racial topics within the existent curriculum of schools, universities, and colleges for the purpose of providing a more accurate examination and presentation of academic subjects. In many instances, multicultural courses are interdisciplinary, and they are coordinated through a specific office or committee. Advocates of ethnic studies and multiculturalism share a concern for addressing the academic and intellectual needs of minority students and for enriching the intellectual and academic experience of those involved in education. They also have to face the charges of using education to promote ethnic and racial separatism and tribalism through indoctrination and for distorting traditional knowledge. Like ethnic studies programs, multicultural education has also been stereotyped as "affirmative action" programs which promote the use of "non-academic political criteria" for hiring and recruiting minority faculty and students.

ON BEING MULTICULTURAL: ADAPTABILITY OR MARGINALITY

The concept "multicultural" has a history that predates the ethnic and racial riots of the 1960s. One of the first explicit uses of the term "multicultural" is found in Edward F. Haskell's 1941 novel *Lance: A Novel About Multicultural*

Men. Written at the beginning of World War II, Haskell tries to provide a "theoretical and cultural solution" to the international conflict. His extensive traveling across Europe put him in direct contact with the difficulties of cultural adaptation. The book tells the story of Lancelot Ternorton, a British scientist, who, during WWI, spent his childhood to the age of sixteen touring the continent as a circus performer. During the tours, he "acquires facilities in various languages and an appreciation of national cultures that is more than skin-deep. He became a "multicultural man," that is, a relativist person for whom "no single social system, nation, creed can ever impose itself on the world as a standard for all peoples."[1] Being multicultural also means having the capacity to put any "social phenomenon . . . under scientific scrutiny and publicly report how the wheels go around."[2] Haskell defines the "multicultural" experience as a positive and liberating mental condition that reinforces a relativist understanding of reality. Through exposure to other cultures, a person develops a "world outlook," and becomes better equipped to adapt himself or herself to changing cultural environments.[3]

While Haskell's multicultured man is a person well-equipped to adapt and survive in society, some sociologists viewed cultural contact as a source of conflict and personal maladjustment. For sociologists such as Robert Park, Loius Wirth, and Everett V. Stonequist living in the midst of multiple cultures creates a "marginal man;" a person who lives in "the cultural life and traditions of two distinct peoples, never quite willing to break, even if we're permitted to do so, with his past and his traditions, and not quite accepted, because of racial prejudice . . ."[4] The personality of the marginal person arises out of a "bi-cultural (or multi-cultural) situation in which members of one group are seeking to adjust themselves to the group which possesses greater prestige and power." Stonequist describes the development of the personality of the marginal man as follows:

> The two cultures produce a dual pattern of identification and a divided loyalty, and the attempt to maintain self-respect transforms these feelings into an ambivalent attitude. The individual may pass in and out of each group situation several times a day; thus his attention is repeatedly focused upon each group attitude and his relationship to it. . . . His racial status is continually called in question; naturally, his attention is turned upon himself to an excessive degree: thus increased sensitiveness, self-consciousness, and race-consciousness, an indefinable *malaise*, inferiority, and various compensatory mechanisms, are common traits in the marginal person.[5]

In Stonequist's analysis, the "natural" response of the marginal man to the strain arising in "multi-cultural" situations ranges from increasing his or her efforts to be accepted by the dominant group to resentment and confrontation with members of the dominant group. For Louis Wirth, these conflicting currents of culture and diverge social codes bidding for the participation and allegiance of its members, explains the relatively high prevalence of crime and delinquency not just among immigrant families, but also in places where cultural "contacts are extended . . . [and] heterogeneous groups mingle. . . ."[6] In order to survive, the marginal person will have to accommodate and assimilate himself or herself to the cultural environment. This natural process will eventually create a new social order based on "stable equilibrium" between competing groups. By the mid-1940s, the idea that differences in values in our "multicultural society contribute to cultural conflict and to juvenile delinquency itself" was widely accepted among many sociologists,[7] and it was used to justify the accommodation and assimilation of minorities within the mainstream culture.

The pathological view of the multicultural environment came to a halt with the publication of *An American Dilemma* in 1944. Specifically, the study debunked the view of accommodation and assimilation as a *laissez-faire* and natural process governing interethnic relationships.[8] As a result, sociologists began to shift their attention to the learning process involved in race and ethnic relations. Studies conducted by psychologists between 1930 and 1950 had shown that interracial relations are based on learned patterns of beliefs, values, and attitudes, which are formed and transformed through our "familiarity with members of the despised race." In addition, by the late 1940s, the idea that biological factors account for racial differences in intelligence and behavior became discredited by Hitler's "final solution policy" for the extermination of the Jewish people. Biological determinism was replaced by the notion that ethnic and racial differences were the product of human interaction with the environment. That meant that social behavior and attitudes were "learned" rather than biologically "innate" attributes of the individual. This paradigm shift expanded and solidified the possibility of reconstructing internal peace and racial harmony within and between nations through education; a solution described by Haskell as the building of "ultramodern multicultural" people.[9] By the 1960s and 1970s, the term "multicultural" has become part of the public discourse to describe inter-subjective understandings between individuals from different cultures and their implications for society and organizations.[10] One also finds the term multicultural loosely used in reference to cultural events, description of communities, and educational programs that involve a diversity of ethnic representations and citizenry.[11] More significantly, multiculturalism became a part of the heated debate between defenders of the Western canon and those whose voices were silenced.

THE GREAT BOOKS MOVEMENT
AND THE MAKING OF THE CANON

To a great extent, the emergence and incorporation of multiculturalism in education came as a response to the dominance of the European classics into the curriculum under the label of the Great Books or the Canon. The ideological and academic impact of the Great Books Movement, led by John Erskine and Mortimer J. Adler, is undeniable. Typically, the list of great books includes those that in one way or another have their roots in work of European writers, particularly from ancient Greek and Roman scholars. In 1928, educator John Erskine, in his book *The Delight of Great Books* argue that what makes a book a "great book" is its immortality, that is, great books call the reader to "read them again and again," and they reveal "the human soul in all places and in all times."[12] In order to discover a great book, the book . . . should be read over and over. Until we have discovered that certain books grow with our maturing experience and other books do not, we have not learned how to distinguish a great book from a book.[13] While at Columbia College, Erskine's designed a General Honors course in classic texts which led to the college's Colloquium on Important Books.[14] Erskine found the support of prominent faculty members, including Mortimer J. Adler, who helped him design the reading list of the "great books" for the General Honors course. In 1930, University of Chicago's President Robert Maynard Hutchins, going against the objection of the philosophy department, recruited Adler to the faculty in that department, and they began editing the fifty-four-volume *Great Books of the Western World Series*.[15] Hutchins and Adler, rejected John Dewey's pragmatic view of education, according to which the scientific method and rational inquiry represent the best learning methods. From this perspective, there is nothing beyond the realm of experience; people learn from experimenting with things and ideas that are of interest to them. Therefore the learning process should be geared toward the scientific examination of what the learner is interested in understanding or has experienced. For Adler, this was an untenable position, for it presupposes that there are no transcendental "truths" to be experienced and discovered before a person become interested in them. In his words,

> . . . there are things that every child has to learn before he can be interested in them; things that we have to learn although we may never be interested in them. There is a less formidable way of saying it: We cannot wait to become interested in brushing our teeth before we are taught to do it."[16]

Adler's main attack on Dewey's pragmatism is its assumption of the superiority of scientific and practical knowledge over philosophical knowledge, specifically moral philosophy. Adler's denies Dewey's modernist view of morals as something separate from reality by arguing that moral principles can be established only in terms of the nature of things as they are; that is, before we can know what should be done, we have to know what is and what is not possible. In other words, moral philosophy cannot be separated from reality, whose ultimate lineaments are the province of theoretical philosophy. Adler, then, uses the above idea to defend his philosophical position that "there is more to life than individual's experience." A person, he argues, "whoever, wherever, whenever, however he is, confronts love and hate, ambition and abnegation and despair, hope, terror, envy, sacrifice, betrayal, temptation, satiety, trust, and mistrust, pleasure and pain, death and dream of eternal life."[17] These are moral dilemmas that exist "outside childhood experience, and yet belong to the preparation of the young for adult life." To learn about these moral dilemmas, children must be given an opportunity to *experience* them through the study of the ideas of the greatest thinkers:

> The child may have to make what for him are terrible choices, but he cannot have to choose between dishonor and death, or integrity and starvation, . . . There may not be martyrs and saints and heroes in a given schoolroom or in a given town or even in a given country or a given decade, but mankind may need martyrs, saints, and heroes a decade later. How is the child in such circumstances to have experience of them so that, if he will not be one of them himself, he will at least know one when he sees him, and not mistake him for a rogue or a fool? Where in the experience of childhood except through the study of the past is the child in such circumstances to acquire "the habitual vision of greatness"?

In Adler's view progressive schools and colleges have been failing "miserably to give students an adequate liberal education"[18] that will prepare them for adult life. During a speech delivered at the Annual Convention of the National Council of Teachers, Adler allegedly told the one thousand teachers of English that the result of this failure "has been the graduation of students who can read no better than six-grade children, who can not write well, or speak well, or listen well."[19] Furthermore, Adler attacked Dewey's pragmatic model of the school system and adult education for its overemphasizing the study of "contemporary problems" at the expense of opening the students' mind to more enduring fundamental problems.

> Progressivism has become so absorbed with the study of the contemporary world that it forgets human culture has traditional roots. It has substituted information for understanding, and science for wisdom. It has mistaken license for liberty, for that is what freedom is when unaccompanied by discipline.[20]

In Adler's view, not only has the schools and colleges failed that students in getting a liberal education but it has also failed in teaching students how to read a book; a fundamental skill to appreciate great books. In his 1940 famous book *How to Read a Book*, Adler argues that to appreciate the "greatness of a book" reading should be a shared experience; a community of people getting together to talk about books they have read.[21] Creating "communities of readers" was Adler's main dream, opening the students' minds was his ultimate goal.

By 1946, Adler and Hutchins's work at the University of Chicago has produced significant programmatic results as evidenced by the coordination of reading groups composed of about six thousand adults in Detroit's public library, the University of Michigan Extension, Wayne University, the University of Detroit, Indiana State Library, Indiana University Extension, Butler University, Indiana, Indiana city public school system, and the Indiana State Association for Adult Education.[22] *The New York Times* described Adler's design of the great books meetings as follows:

> None of the participants will pay fess, nor will they enroll in any institution. Their instructors will be non-professional volunteers, who are being trained without charge in the techniques of leading discussion. The training is given by a traveling staff of University of Chicago lecturers and instructors headed by Mortimer J. Adler, Professor of the Philosophy of Law. The movement is an outgrowth of the "great books" classes offered at the university by Chancellor Robert M. Hutchins and Professor Adler. . . . At the present time, 330 leaders—men and women—are attending training classes in the four cities. These discussion leaders include businessmen, workers, librarians, teachers, newspapermen, lawyers, and doctors.[23]

Adler's goal was the expansion of the Great Books project to reach "a universal adult education program, involving sixty million men and women, to develop competent citizens in the United States."[24] By 1947, the Great Books Movement has outgrown the experimental project stage, and Hutchins and Adler incorporated the Great Books Foundation as a not-for-profit educational organization. On April 30, 1950, members of the Great Books foundation announced the celebration the thirtieth birthday of the Columbia's Colloquium on Important Books that led to the formation of the Great Books movement. *The New York Times* described the event as "a gala birthday party," to celebrate the birth of the Colloquium and to honor Professor Erskine.

> If he is well enough to attend, Professor Erskine will be singled out for special honors. It was his notion thirty years ago that barriers of language should not be allowed to interfere with students' appreciation of living (or not-so-living) classics and this principle still guides the course. Columbia College planners agree only tomorrow's celebration at the Men's Faculty Club . . . promises to be as delightful and full of surprises as any Colloquium sessions. They plan to sing

"Happy Birthday" and will toast a "many, many more" to what they consider to be a truly "living" course."[25]

The incorporation of the Great Books as not-for-profit organization coincided with the efforts of Paul G. Hoffman, first president of the Ford Foundation, to expand the operations of the Foundation. Hoffman priority was the decentralization of the foundation to "get results quickly and . . . on a large scale," by subcontracting services. On April 23, 1951, the Foundation announced the creation of the Fund for Adult Education (FAE), whose main goal was "expanding opportunities for people to continue their education throughout adult life." C. Scott Fletcher, president of Encyclopedia Britannica Films, was appointed president of the FAE. Members of the new organization agreed that the FAE "would focus exclusively on liberal adult education." Unquestionably, Adler's Great Books organization fitted the FAE's mission perfectly, and received a grant for $175,000 from the organization for "the expansion of the foundation's program for training leaders of community discussion groups."[26] According to the FAE's ten-year report (1951–1961):

> The Fund for Adult Education provided the [Great Books] Foundation substantial yearly support from May 1950 to July 1960. In 1959 it made an additional grant of half a million dollars for operations beyond 1960. This grant was conditional on the Foundation's raising a matching sum of $500,000 from other sources. It was estimated that this million dollars, combined with the income from book sales, membership and miscellaneous sources, would see the Foundation through to the time when 100,000 persons would be actively engaged in its programs, and its financial position would be secure. . . . The Great Books foundation obtained cash and pledges for the matching sum and received the Fund's grant.[27]

By 1952, Adler has reached such a high level of prominence that *Time Magazine* dedicated its cover page and a full-length article to him titled, "Fusilier." The following passage reveals the tone of the article:

> He started as an undergraduate at Columbia over 30 years ago. Professor John Dewey, then the Jove of Morningside Heights, once came to a meeting of the university philosophy club to hear one of his students read a paper. As the thin, intense young man warmed to his subject, the great philosopher's face grew red. Finally, when young Adler quoted a passage from Dewey and commented, "There is certainly nothing of the love of God in this utterance," Dewey could take no more. He jumped to his feet shouting, "Nobody is going to tell me how to love God," and stalked out. In class, Mortimer Adler harassed the eminent professor by sending him long, learned letters pointing out how his lectures contradicted his earlier lectures. For a time, pragmatist Dewey read the letters in class, but eventually, he called Adler to his office and suggested he lay off.

Adler did not lay off. He has continued to take intellectual potshots at Dewey and his disciples. Socrates with Dry Martini. This target practice has won him a unique position in U.S. education.[28]

The magnitude of the work of the Great Books Foundation was reflected in their publication of the encyclopedia *Great Books of the Western World*, which took approximately "nine years and $2,000,000" to produce.[29]

THE WORK OF THE GREAT BOOKS MOVEMENT

At the core of the Great Books Foundation program was the discussion groups; individuals who met in public libraries and other public places to discuss "selected readings of central importance in our civilization" that ranged from the Declaration of Independence to Freud's works.[30] By 1960, the Great Books program had over 42,000 participants in more than 1,100 communities.[31] While other adult education programs were based on Dewey's progressive and pragmatic pedagogy, the Great Books programs were aimed at imparting and reinforcing Western values and ideas among the American people.

Between 1956 and 1958, the National Opinion Research Center (NOPC) conducted a series of evaluations Great Books groups based on a sample of 1909 participants. Among other things, the study found that participants in the Great Books programs "tended to be well educated, of high status, socially active, and young," and they were not

> "ivory-tower intellectuals," but rather show "middlebrow" intellectual interests; and far for being alienated from their society, they share its middle-class values and norms of community participation. Neither are they "social misfits," for the old and the unmarried (people for whom society often has no niche) are underrepresented. . . .[32]

The NOPC's data also indicated that the groups had "a slight disproportion of females," particularly "housewives." Over-femininity was interpreted as "not a good sign" because "it was associated with lower activity in discussion, and . . . groups with high proportions of women have greater loss rates."[33] When asked about their primary motivation to join the great books program, the study found that although the program attracts people with a wide variety of motivations, "the focus is not intellectual (learning what the great minds have to say), but rather on specific skills and techniques, and—we hate to say it—gimmicks." Specifically, the majority of the participants saw their participation in the program as a stepping stone for success in other areas (e.g., improving leadership skills, job skills, and group discussion skills). Further, the attempt at making the discussion groups a place where people read the great books and questioned each other's ideas and opinions faced many challenges. The study found that "as they sit around table, in spite of any differences in sex, job, religion, age, generation, etc., most of the people will be talking with others who have pretty much the same aims, and very much will they be talking across the table to someone who has a radically different conception of the purposes of the program." Finally, 55 percent of the participants said that they had enjoyed some parts of the Great Books program, "but on the whole, I can't say it changed me very much."[34] However, the study found that

> Continued exposure to Great Books does seem to affect intellectual orientations toward religions and also seems to lead to change in certain political positions. The religious trends appear to be in the direction of greater acceptance of liberal and skeptical approaches to religion, without, however, abandonment of prior religious faith. The political trend is toward "18th-century liberalism," (or perhaps new conservatism) defined as increased concern about civil liberties combined with opposition to government controls in other areas.[35]

One year after the survey, the NOPC conducted a follow-up study to determine the drop-out rates of the groups in the original sample. The results were discouraging since "about one third lost more than half of their members, including 17 percent which succumbed; about one third lost between 30 percent and 50 percent of their original members; a little less than one third kept more than 70 percent of their members." Further, the study indicated that the Great Books programs tend to retain "not those who need the most intellectual grow, but those whose preparation and interest are already strong."[36] The fact that the study did not include race is an indication that perhaps the programs did not target this population, or that the program did not appeal to members of minority groups. By the late 1960s, the efforts at addressing the education needs of the masses had left untouched the precarious conditions of the minority population. Drawing from the activism of the civil rights movement and the international pressure for decolonization, some radical leaders, dissatisfied workers, and students denounced the exploitative and colonizing nature of the Eurocentric education system in the United States. It was within this context that multiculturalism was conceived as a plan to decolonize and liberate minority people nationally and internationally.[37]

THE GREAT BOOKS MOVEMENT FACES MULTICULTURAL EDUCATION

One of the most significant steps in the institutionalization of "multicultural education" took place on February 1970 when the American Association of Colleges for Teacher Education (AACTE) established the Commission on Multicultural Education to investigate and promote the inclusion of multicultural education in the preparation of teachers. Two years later, the Commission issued the multicultural statement "No One Model American." The statement contained the following principles:

> Multicultural education is education which values cultural pluralism. Multiculturalism rejects the view that schools should seek to melt away cultural differences or the view that schools should merely tolerate cultural pluralism. . . . It affirms that major education institutions should strive to preserve and enhance cultural pluralism. To endorse cultural pluralism is to endorse the principle that there is no one model American. . . . Cultural pluralism rejects both assimilation and separatism as ultimate goals. . . . Colleges and universities engaged in the preparation of teachers have a central role in the positive development of our culturally pluralistic society. Evidence [of multicultural education] . . . includes such factors as a faculty and staff of multiethnic and multiracial character, a student body that is representative of the culturally diverse nature of the community being served, and a culturally pluralistic curriculum . . .[38]

In 1976, the National Council for Accreditation of Teacher Education (NCATE), adopted the principles established by the AACTE's Commission on Multicultural Education and incorporated them into their revised Standard for the Accreditation of Teacher Education. The new accreditation standard required that effective January 1979 all "programs for preparing teachers must include multicultural education to prepare personnel to work in a multicultural society."[39] The NCATE defined the scope of multicultural education for prospective teachers as follows:

> Multicultural education is preparation for the social, political and economic realities that individuals experience in culturally diverse and complex human encounters. These realities have both national and international dimensions. Multicultural education could include but not be limited to the experiences which: (1) promote analytical and evaluative abilities to confront issues such as participatory democracy, racism and sexism, and the parity of power; (2) develop skills for values clarification including the study of the manifest and latent transmission of values; (3) examine the dynamics of diverse cultures and the implications for developing teaching strategies; and (4) examine linguistic

variations and diverse learning styles as a basis for the development of appropriate teaching strategies.

The primary goal of the NCATE multicultural standard was to prepare future teachers in the pedagogy of multicultural education as a tool for individual and social change. The NCATE standard specified that although multicultural education emanates from the philosophy of pluralism, which recognizes the existence of numerous ethnic groups, it also includes the analysis of those cultural elements that are common to all groups in society. Moreover, multicultural curricula must address the learning needs of all students regardless of their cultural background. According to the standard, multicultural education is not compensatory or supplemental; instead, it is to be incorporated into all aspects of education, including: "governance, curricula, faculty, students, resources and facilities, and evaluation program review, and planning." The NCATE board made it clear that teacher education programs had an obligation to train prospective teachers for "the social, political, and economic realities that individuals experience in culturally diverse and complex human encounters."[40] Moreover, prospective teachers are expected to develop the necessary analytical and evaluative skills to confront issues such as racism, sexism, the parity of power, the politics of the hidden curriculum, and values clarification.

Between 1977 and 1978, the American Association of Colleges for Teacher Education conducted a survey to determine the extent of multicultural education among public and private universities and colleges. Of the 446 institutions that responded to the survey, 362 institutions (81.2 percent) indicated that they have "some provision for addressing multicultural and bilingual education within the education unit."[41] According to the study, a set of interrelated factors contributed to the planning, development, and implementation of multicultural education at the 362 institutions, including university administrative support, presence of various ethnic groups, state education regulations and legislation, and federal legislation. However, at the same time about a third of the respondents mentioned lack of qualified faculty, curricular material, and funds as "deterrent" to developing and implementing multicultural education in their teacher education programs. As a result, for the most part, multicultural courses and programs were often interdisciplinary and housed within the teacher education schools. This characteristic of multicultural education programs is consistent with the fact that "less than 10 percent of the institutions [surveyed] had a separate department or division of multicultural education (7.4 percent) or bilingual education (8.1 percent)."[42] Also significant was the findings that 45 percent of the institutions in the study had departments or divisions that focused on U.S. ethnic groups, particularly on African American studies, and 60.9 percent of these institutions offered courses related to women's studies. Only 10.4 percent and 7.2 percent of the responding institutions offered courses dealing with Western European Americans and Jewish Americans, respectively. The overall aim of the multicultural programs surveyed and others alike was to "train future leaders within the field and disseminate their talents and abilities on a national level."[43]

Like ethnic studies activists, the AACTE and the NCATE were concerned with "more than merely documenting a people's presence, they were committed to...changing institutional arrangements which dehumanized people of color."[44] Their goal was to use multicultural education as an "intervention and on-going assessment process to help institutions and individuals become more responsive to the human condition, individual cultural integrity, and cultural pluralism in society."[45] Or more radically, creating the "conditions for students to think and act otherwise, to imagine beyond the given, and to critically embrace their identities as a source of agency and possibility."[46]

NOTES

1. "Lance." *The New York Times*, By Edward F. Haskell, (New York: The John Day Company), 1941. Book Review, July 27, 1941, p. 7. Lancelot meets Eleonora Halley, an American communist and her South African-born uncle Bruce Campbell, in Berlin. After years of separation, they meet again in Bulgaria and Eleonora encourages them to become members of the Communist Party and to move with her to Russia to join the Bolshevik revolution. Drawing from his multicultural experience in the Continent, Lancelot "resolutely . . . declines to make the total surrender of free will that party membership involves." Similarly, Bruce Campbell declines the offer and counsels Eleonora to "Go instead to America and get a broader view of the world." In Haskell's novel, Lance and Bruce symbolize the "multicultured men."

2. Ibid., p. 16

3. Ibid.

4. Everet V. Stonequist, "The Problem of the Marginal Man," *The American Journal of Sociology*, July 1935, Vol. XLI, No. 1, p. 1.

5. Ibid., p. 6.

6. Louis Wirth, "Culture and Delinquency: Culture Conflict and Misconduct," *Social Forces*, 1931, Vol. 9, No. 4, p. 488.

7. Harry Manuel Shulman, "The Family and Juvenile Delinquency." *Annals of the American Academy of Political and Social Science*. January 1949, Vol. 261, p. 26.

8. See, Gunnar Myrdal, *An American Dilemma*, p. 1048–1049.

9. Haskell, *Lance: A Novel About Multicultural Men*, p.331.

10. Raymond M. Hainer, "Rationalism, Pragmatism, and Existentialism: Perceived but Undiscovered Multicultural Problems," in (ed.) Evelyn Glatt and Maynard W. Shelly, *The Research Society* (New York: Gordon and Breach), 1968, p. 8

11. "The Made-in-U.S. Label Blankets Western Europe," *The New York Times*, November 24, 1967; *The New York Times*, "Summer Program of State Fairs," August 3, 1969; *The New York Times*, "Court bars San Francisco Delay on a Desegregation Busing Plan," August 13, 1971. *Time*, "New Tides in the Pacific," Friday 26, 1965.

12. John Erskine, *The Delight of Great Books*, (Indianapolis: Bobbs-Merrill Company), 1928, p. 11.

13. Ibid., p. 29 and p. 297.

14. John Erskine. http://c250.columbia.edu/c250_celebrates/remarkable_columbians/john_erskine.html (accessed November 21, 2008).

15. Mortimer J. Adler. *Papers, Special Collections Research Center*, University of Chicago Library. http://ead.lib.uchicago.edu/view.xqy?id=ICU.SPCL.ADLERM&c=a&sub=Adler,%20Mortimer%20Jerome,%201902- (accessed November 21, 2008).

16. Mortimer Adler and Milton Mayer, *The Revolution in Education* (Chicago: University of Chicago Press), 1958, p. 177.

17. Ibid., p. 169.

18. "Educational Duty of Movies Denied," *The New York Times*, January 22, 1938, p. 17.

19. "Asserts Teachers Hamper Education: Dr. Adler Tells English Group They Should Lead Withdrawal of All," *The New York Times*, November 23, 1940, p. 32.

20. "Modern Teaching Termed Confusing: Progressive Trend Stressing Contemporary Problems is Scored by Adler," *The New York Times*, November 12, 1939, p. 24.

21. Mortimer J. Adler, *How to Read a Book: The Art of Getting a Liberal Education*, (New York: Simon and Schuster), 1940.

22. "Great Books Classes in 4 Cities: Leaders in Training," *The New York Times*, May 26, 1946, p. E7.

23. Ibid., p. E7.

24. "Urges Adults to Get Broad Education: Dr. Adler of Chicago Would Develop citizens Through Use of the Great Books," *The New York Times*, June 21, 1946, p. 25.

25. "Book Symposium to Mark Birthday," *The New York Times*, April 9, 1950, p. 59.

26. "Great Books Fund Gets $175,000," *The New York Times*, May 28, 1951, p. 32.

27. Fund for Adult Education, A Ten-Year Report of the Fund for Adult Education, 1951–1961. (New York: FAE), 1962), p. 30.

28. "Fusilier," *Time Magazine*, Monday, March 17, 1952.

29. "54-Volume Summary of Western Culture Hailed as History-Making at Dinner Here," *The New York Times*, April 16, 1952, p. 25.

30. Fund for Adult Education: A Ten-Year Report of the Fund for Adult Education, 1951–1961. pp. 9–10.

31. Ibid., 1962, p. 30.

32. James A. Davis, "A Study of Participants in the Great Books Program." (Chicago: National Opinion Research Center). 1960. ERIC Document, ED028371.

33. James A. Davis, *Great Books and Small Groups*, (New York: Free Press), 1961, p. 221.

34. Ibid., p. 12.

35. Ibid., p. 109.

36. Ibid., p. 217.

37. See, Ivan Illich, *Deschooling Society* (New York: Harper & Row), 1970; Paulo Freire, *Pedagogy of the Oppressed* (New York: Continuum Publishing Corporation), 1970; Albert Memmi, *The Colonizer and the Colonized* (New York: Orion Press), 1965; Frantz Fanon, *Black Skin, White Masks* (New York: Grove Press), [1952] 1967.

38. William A. Hunter, *Multicultural Education Through Competency-Based Teacher Education*, (Washington, DC: AACTE), 1974, p. 21.

39. H. Prentice Baptiste, *Multicultural Teacher Education: Preparing Educators to Provide Educational Equity*, (Washington, DC: AACTE), 1980, p. 2.

40. American Association of Colleges for Teacher Education, *Multicultural Teacher Education: Guidelines for Implementation, Volume IV.* Prepared by Frank H. Klassen, Donna M. Gollnick, and Kobla I. M. Osayande. (Washington, DC: AACTE), 1980, p. 2.

41. Donna M. Gollnick and Jack Levy, *Multicultural Teacher Education: Case Studies of Thirteen Programs.* (Washington, DC: American Association of Colleges for Teacher Education) 1980, p. 7. See also Donna M. Gollnick, *Multicultural Education in Teacher Education: The State of the Scene.* (Washington, DC: American Association of Colleges for Teacher Education), 1978.

42. Ibid., p. 8.

43. Ibid., p. 102.

44. John M. Liu, "Asian American Studies and the Disciplining of Ethnic Studies." In *Frontiers of Asian American Studies*, (ed.) Gail M. Nomura, Russell Endo, Stephen H. Sumida, and Russell C. Leong, (WA: Washington State University Press), 1989, p. 281.

45. Ibid., p. 3.

46. Henry A. Giroux, "Insurgent Multiculturalism," (ed) David Theo Goldberg, *Multiculturalism: A Critical Reader*, (Cambridge, MA: Blackwell), 1994, p. 328.

Chapter Five

Theorizing About Multiculturalism

During the 1980s and 1990s, multiculturalism in education became the subject of philosophical and theoretical analysis outside the field of teacher education. There was a shift in emphasis from multicultural education as a "system-based product" to multicultural education as a "political process" linked to issues of individual and group identity. During the institutionalization phase of multicultural education, there was an emphasis on how to implement multicultural education. Based on a body of literature supporting the argument that ethnicity affects the learning process, many educators assumed that incorporating cultural studies within the curriculum and the classrooms would enhance the academic achievement of minority students, and at the same time it would improve the self-esteem of minority students as well as intercultural relationships in society. With the assistance of federal, state, and private contributions, a large amount of financial and time resources were spent in producing curricular material, and conducting seminars and workshops dealing with the implementation of multicultural education. Particularly significant was the proliferation of multicultural education resource manuals to assist teachers and schools in locating and purchasing curricular material for reducing prejudice and celebrating ethnic differences. In many schools, there was a strong emphasis on the ethnically-based four "Fs"—Facts, Foods, Famous People, and Festivals. The ultimate goal was to produce a culturally integrated learning environment that would enhance the learning process and at the same time would recognize and respect the humanness and dignity of all people.[1]

By the mid-1980s, the limitations of the "four Fs" approach to multicultural education became evident. The approach was problematic and insufficient "because it too often emphasizes isolated facts about famous people [and facts] and does not help children to develop higher level thinking skills or to learn how to resolve value-related personal and social problems." As critical multiculturalist James Banks puts it:

> Some teachers view multiethnic [multicultural] education primarily as the study of the "strange" and "exotic" customs and behavior of ethnic groups and as the celebration of ethnic holidays and birthdays. Teachers who view multiethnic education in this way often have students build tepees and igloos, and make and eat ethnic foods such as chitlins, enchiladas, and chow mein. . . . Some schools have Black week, Indian day and Chicano "afternoon." On these special occasions, students prepare ethnic foods, build tepees, venerate ethnic "heroes," sing ethnic songs, and perform ethnic dances. Ethnic community people might also be invited to the school to give talks that "tell like it is". . . . By focusing on the experiences of ethnic groups only on special days and holidays, teachers are likely to reinforce the notion that ethnic groups are not integral parts of American society and culture. Students are likely to conclude that "Black history" and "American history" are separate things. . . . Focusing on the "strange and exotic" traits and characteristics of ethnic groups is likely to reinforce stereotypes and misconceptions. The making of tepees does not reveal anything significant about contemporary American Indian values, cultures or experiences. It merely adds to the classical Indian stereotype, which is so pervasive on television and in wider society.[2]

Evidently, in many schools administrators and teachers obviated the NCATE's conceptualization of multicultural education which stresses the development of "analytical and evaluative abilities to confront issues such as participatory democracy, racism and sexism, and the parity of power." Instead, many schools adopted the more liberal "four-Fs" approach to multiculturalism.

CRITICAL MULTICULTURALISM

During the late 1980s, a group of critical multiculturalists, particularly from Canada, challenged the "four F's" approach by suggesting that it should be replaced by a multicultural model in which events and situations are examined from different perspectives of which the Anglo-American perspectives "are only one group of several." Prompted by the above pedagogical concern a new body of literature emerged that advanced a critical and "social reconstructionist" view of multicultural education. From this perspective, "multicultural education should prepare students to deal with race, class, and gender oppression in society, and to take charge of their life circumstances."[3] This critical and intersectional view of multicultural education was consistent with the National Council for Accreditation of Teacher Education's definition of multicultural education which specified that "multicultural education could include but not be limited to the experiences that . . . promote analytical and evaluative abilities to confront issues such as participatory democracy, racism and sexism, and the parity of power." NCATE's multicultural mandate also indicated that "designers of multicultural education programs must be cognizant of concepts that describe the relationship or interactions among individuals and groups. These concepts are racism, sexism, prejudice, discrimination, oppression, powerlessness, power, inequality, equality, and stereotypes."[4] The incorporation of these concepts within the school curriculum, at all levels, requires a critical view of multicultural education.

Borrowing from the literature on postmodernism and liberation pedagogy the school of critical multiculturalism stresses the need to empower teachers and students through a strategy of oppositional "discourse," whereby students and teachers have

> . . . a legitimate voice to contest and critique educational policy and practice. It requires that teachers and students develop the confidence and competence to speak what has previously been unspoken, to identify sources of individual and collective oppression, and to work to eliminate them. In policy and practice the focus of multicultural education would be on developing a discourse that illuminates a greater understanding of the self and the multiple ascribed characteristics (ethnicity, gender, socioeconomic status) that are used to define how institutions work, their histories of exploitation and repression. It further means, . . . [that] the classroom becomes the site not merely of an individual's apprehension of his or her own experience, but a place where there is a collective reinterpretation of our lived world. There is, in other words the making of a communal culture that opposes that which is hegemonic. . . .[5]

At the center of critical multiculturalism is the idea that any "discourse" contains and defines within itself its own objects and subjects at the expense of excluding others. Helping students identify and understand how a dominant body of knowledge emerges provides them with an opportunity to examine how "knowledge" shapes and maintain power relationships. Students will learn how privileges and rights are controlled through the hegemonic discourse which provides the framework for understanding the authority and legitimacy of what is said and not said. From a critical multicultural perspective, educators must be aware that education is not neutral, the decision as to what to teach implies a decision as to what to exclude. Hence, it is the role of the educator to give voice to those members of society whose contribution to society has been silenced within mainstream society. Furthermore, educators must also understand that when they claim to be taking "a neutral position or offers a neutral discourse" in the classroom, "he or she is merely presenting a perspective."[6]

One of the most influential members of the critical school of multiculturalism is Peter McLaren who has referred to the prevalent institutionalized forms of multicultural education as "conservative or corporate multiculturalism." As he explains:

> Although they would like officially to distance themselves from racist ideologies, conservative multiculturalists pay only lip service to the cognitive equality of all races and charge unsuccessful minorities with having "culturally deprived backgrounds" and a "lack of strong family-oriented values." This "environmentalist" position still accepts black cognitive inferiority to whites as a general premise and provides conservative multiculturalists with a means of rationalizing why some minority groups are successful while other groups are not. This also gives the white cultural elite the excuse they need for unreflectively and disproportionately occupying positions of power. . . . conservative or corporate multiculturalism refuses to treat whiteness as a form of ethnicity and in doing so posits whiteness as invisible norm by which other ethnicities are judged.[7]

Similarly, for critical multiculturalists, conservative multiculturalism reinforces the centrality of the Eurocentric curriculum by presenting the contribution of ethnic minorities to the mainstream society as "add-ons to the dominant culture." The hidden curriculum within conservative multicultural education reinforces the pluralistic vision of a harmonious and nationally united society based on ethnic tolerance and respect without critically questioning knowledge-based power relations. Moreover, conservative multiculturalism uncritically operates within the pedagogical limits established by the education system with its emphasis on the search for "objective truth" at the expense of a subjective and dialogical search for justice and freedom.

At a different, yet interrelated, level critical multiculturalists call our attention to the way "differences" and "identities" are produced through the manipulation of the socially and politically defined cultural signs. Specifically, following a deconstructionist perspective, critical multiculturalists emphasize the importance of language in organizing the self, groups, and social practices. From this perspective, the view of the ethnic studies movement, for instance, as an expression of angered and frustrated minorities takes a different meaning: it is not longer perceived as a mere struggle for power or revenge but as a process of self-definition and identity building, that is, as a group of people exercising their right to define themselves. St. Clair Drake has used this perspective to explain the internal logic of the black studies movement:

> The primary goal of the black studies movement during its early stages was to utilize the classroom as well as extra-curricular activities for raising the consciousness and heightening as the group pride of black students so that they would be transformed from "Negroes," anxious to be integrated, into "blacks,"

convinced that "black is beautiful" and ready to struggle for Black Power. The need for self-definition was considered urgent at predominantly white universities and colleges because there were so few black role models functioning as administrators, professors, or counselors, and the white middle class was dominant.[8]

Philosophically, critical multiculturalism borrows from Paulo Freire's notion of the pedagogy of the oppressed to base its humanitarian and emancipatory claims. As an advocate of cultural and literacy programs in developing countries, Freire proposed that education should be concerned with restoring the lost "humanized" nature of the oppressed and their oppressors.[9] However, for Freire the oppressed must always define and control the terms and the strategies that will guide the process of human liberation. Historically, some liberated oppressors (e.g., teachers, business leaders, politicians) will side with the oppressed, however, these alliance must always be critically examined because liberated oppressors

> always bring with them the marks of their origin: their prejudices and their deformations, which include a lack of confidence in the people's ability to think, to want, and to know. Accordingly, these adherents to the people's cause constantly run the risk of falling into a type of generosity as malefic as that of the oppressors.[10]

Not having developed a critical understanding of reality, some of these liberated oppressors will continue to perceive the oppressed as "marginal" and "pathological" people whose way of thinking prevent them from full integration into a healthy and just society. The oppressed must learn to be suspicious of those oppressors who side with them with the implicit intention of social integration. As Freire indicates, the purpose of "conscientization" is not to integrate the oppressed into the structure of oppression, but to transform it so that they can be "beings for themselves."[11]

Following Freire's analysis, critical multiculturalists see education as a tool for deconstructing the binary category of white and black by making whiteness a visible sign.

> It [critical multiculturalism] challenges meaning systems that impose attributes on the Other under the direction of sovereign signifiers and tropes. And this means not directing all our efforts at understanding ethnicity as "other than white," but interrogating the culture of whiteness itself. This is crucial because unless we do this—unless we give white students a sense of their own identity as an emergent ethnicity—we naturalize whiteness as a cultural marker against which Otherness is defined. Coco Fusco warns that "To ignore white ethnicity is to redouble its hegemony by naturalizing it. Without specifically addressing

white ethnicity there can be no critical evaluation of the construction of the other." White groups need to examine their own ethnic histories so that they are less likely to judge their own cultural norms as neutral and universal. The supposed neutrality of white culture enables it to commodify blackness to its own advantage and ends. It allows it to manipulate the "other" but not see this "otherness" as a white tool of exploitation.[12]

Bringing whiteness to the center of multicultural critique would take white people out of their self-demarked "comfort zone" and would make them visible to themselves and to the "others."

Critical multiculturalists accuse traditional multiculturalists of overemphasizing the "subordinate" position of a minority groups and their deficits. Henry A. Giroux's insurgent multiculturalism addresses this concern:

> . . . a critical multiculturalism must shift attention away from an exclusive focus on subordinate groups . . . to one that examines how racism in its various forms is produced semiotically, and institutionally at various levels of society. . . . [A] critical analysis of race must move beyond the discourse of blaming the victim in which whites view multiculturalism as a code word for black lawlessness and other "problems" blacks create for white America. Viewing black people in this manner reveals not only white supremacy as the discursive and institutional face of racism, but it also presents us with the challenge of addressing racial issues not as a dilemma of black people but as a problem endemic to the legacy [of] colonialism rooted in historical inequalities and longstanding cultural stereotypes.[13]

From the above perspective, a critical multicultural curriculum must go beyond the traditional celebration of differences by taking on the challenge of creating democratic spaces in school where issues of individual and collective identity and their politics are openly and critically examined, debated and redefined. In Giroux's insurgent multiculturalism the institution of education becomes an extension of democratic life, and a site for interrogating present conditions of injustices and engaging in its transformation.

In addition to the above critiques of conservative or traditional multicultural education, critical multiculturalists question the official politics of recognition embedded in institutionalized multicultural education programs which uncritically accepts a "presumption of equal worth" of all cultural practices. The argument made by traditional multiculturalists is that the Eurocentric biases within the "canon" must be eliminated to make it more accurate and inclusive of the contributions of marginalized and excluded people. The ultimate goal is not just expanding the body of knowledge of the students, but equally important to help members of the excluded groups in building a sense of self-worth through curricular inclusion and recognition of their equal worth. Although critical multiculturalists welcome such a noble purpose, they argue that when taken as an "act of faith," in practice the presumption of equal worth has the potential to turn multicultural education into a "condescending and patronizing" pedagogy. More often than not, non-canonical works are included in the "canon" without seriously confronting them with the established canonical knowledge. Recognizing the impossibility of having an objective standard of "worthiness" against to which we can evaluate cultural products and ideas, Charles Taylor indicates that:

> ... real judgments of worth suppose a fused horizon of standards ... they suppose that we have been transformed by the study of the other, so that we are not simply judging by our original familiar standards. A favorable judgment made prematurely would be not only condescending but ethnocentric. It would praise the other for being like us. ... The peremptory demand for favorable judgments of worth is paradoxically—perhaps one should say tragically—homogenizing. For it implies that we already have the standards to make such judgments.[14]

Taylor's proposed "fusion of horizons" is aimed at teaching and learning how "to move in a broader horizon, within which what we have formerly taken from granted as the background to valuation can be situated as one possibility alongside the different background of the formerly unfamiliar culture."[15] Hence, rather than "inclusion by demand" there should be a demand for a rigorous and intensive study of all cultures. Through this process, taken-for-granted standards of worth are constantly challenged, contrasted and transformed.

Will Kymlicka provides a more radical theoretical critique of institutionalized multiculturalism by suggesting that it does not go far enough in advancing and protecting the rights of minority groups to have political representation and self-government. The main argument is that the incorporation of minority members into the mainstream culture erodes the foundation of identity, self-worth, and self-respect of its members; a process that reinforces their subordinate status. Therefore, the state should play an active role in advancing policies to protect the rights of minority groups to maintain their culture. Governmental intervention is justified on the ground that liberal democracy implies the right of individuals as well as groups to maintain and protect their culture within the larger society. It is also justified as an act of justice, for it protects the cultural and institutional framework which allows minority people to understand reality according to their own moral standards.

In Kymlicka's view, culture "provides its members with meaningful ways of life across a wide range of human activities, including social, educational, religious, recreational and economic life, encompassing both public and private spheres."[16] This claim makes Kymlicka's defense of multiculturalism problematic. It is clear that for Kymlicka cultural membership is the primary and dominant source of identity and self-worth for minorities. Such reductionist view renders his analysis as sociologically deterministic. The primacy of culture and group membership in Kymlicka's thesis contradicts his liberal defense of individualism and freedom. In 1964 Milton Gordon expressed this dilemma by observing that:

> While the doctrine of cultural pluralism claims to be truly democratic because it allows each ethnic group to maintain its communality and culture, how democratic is it if is presented in such a categorical fashion that each individual must remain within the structural and cultural confines of his "birthright" ethnic group regardless of his wishes in the matter? To put the issue more succinctly, while cultural pluralism may be democratic for groups, how democratic is it for individuals?[17]

Gordon's concern has hunted pluralism and multiculturalism for decades. In dealing with the issue, Kymlicka makes a distinction between group rights aimed at "external protection" and those rights which limit "internal restrictions." The former group of rights are intended to protect the minority groups against the political, economic, and cultural power of the larger society, whereas the second set of rights is intended to protect the right of individuals within the group to question, revise, or abandon aspects of their original culture (patriarchy, FGM, sexism, and so on). In Kymlicka's view, both sets of group rights are consistent with liberal democracy for they recognize the autonomy of groups and individuals.[18]

Recently, Brian Walker and other contemporary theorists have rejected the "all-encompassing" view of culture and ethnic membership. Such claim, critics argue, becomes highly questionable in light of the influence of the mass media and technology on one's identity and sense of self-worth besides ethnicity.[19] As Brian Walker indicates, "the supposedly foundational cultural traits we pick up within our ethnic communities are frequently overriding by the norms of these institutions we live and work in."[20] Again, this criticism does not invalidate Kymlicka's theory of multiculturalism for it contains a defense of the right of individuals to voluntarily abandon some aspects of their group culture, and adopting those of the larger society that he or she deems important or valuable.

Another criticism of multiculturalism in all of its manifestations suggests that it places to much of emphasis on culture "to the detriment of more important issues," such as class and gender inequalities. In so doing, traditional multiculturalism "mystifies and mitigates state representation of the real interests of minority groups."[21] That is, by focusing on non-controversial and exotic aspects of culture such as food, language, clothes, dance, music, traditional multiculturalism neutralizes and perpetuates economic inequality between and within ethnic groups.[22] To illustrate, feminist scholar Susan Moller Okin finds it difficult to reconcile any form of multiculturalism that is based on an uncritical claim to protect minority groups in which women are exploited and oppressed. As she points out:

> In many of the cultural groups that now form significant minorities in the United States, Canada, and Europe, families place girls under significantly greater constraint than their brothers. They restrict their dress, participation in extracurricular and social activities, unchaperoned dating, further education, choice of employment, choice of spouse, and time of marriage. . . . It is therefore, difficult to understand how these young women's cultures could be viewed as providing for them the background enabling them "to make informed decisions about how to lead their lives," "to make choices amongst various meaningful options," or "to freely pursue the life they see fit"—functions that liberal defenders of multiculturalism ascribe to cultures.[23]

Sarah Song has shown how the ideology of multiculturalism may lead to gender-based injustices within the courtroom. For instance, the case of *Santa Clara Pueblo v. Martinez (1975)* involved Audrey Martinez who was raised within the tribe and who was denied membership in the tribe because her mother married outside the tribe. According to a tribal rule only men who married outside the tribe could pass their membership to their children. Upon examination, the Supreme Court decided that it could not hear the equal protection claim because it implies an undue interference by the Court with the right of the Pueblo community to "maintain itself as a culturally and politically distinct entity." In *People v. Chen* (1988) based on the expert testimony of an anthropologist who argued that violence against unfaithful spouses was part of the Chinese culture, the trial judge sentenced Dong Lu Chen to "5 years' probation" rather than to the applicable prison sentence for second-degree murder.[24] Empirical cases like those examined by Song clearly show the tension between multiculturalism and feminism, and the need to include an internal critical analysis of how minority cultures reinforce structural traditional patriarchal inequalities within groups as part of the multicultural agenda. However, as Song argues, this internal critical analysis of minority cultures does not imply an endorsement of minority assimilation into the mainstream culture as a way of protecting the rights of minority individuals because "the majority culture is in certain respects not less patriarchal than minority cultures."[25]

THE ANTI-MULTICULTURALIST MOVEMENT IN THE UNITED STATES

Since its inception, multiculturalism, in its liberal and critical forms, faced bitter opposition from many camps, and by the mid-1990s, the arguments against multiculturalism have become very well articulated. One of the most common attacks on multiculturalism was predicated on the perceived threat that multiculturalism, with its emphasis on ethnic identity, represents for the "national identity." This reaction is traceable to the anti-pluralist position of melting-pot advocates for whom the preservation of ancestral cultural traits and values by immigrants represents an impediment to the formation and preservation of national identity, unity and harmony. Others have attacked multiculturalism on the grounds that in its attempt at promoting curricular inclusion, multicultural educators have engaged in a distortion of history and in the process they have diluted the education process by deemphasizing the study of Western thought. What follows is a brief examination of some the work produced by some leading anti-multiculturalists.

From an academic standpoint, in 1984 Williams Bennett launched a direct attack on multiculturalism with the publication of *To Reclaim a Legacy: A Report on the Humanities in Higher Education*. The report was based on the input provided by a study group organized by Bennett and composed of "thirty-one prominent teachers, scholars, administrators, and authorities on higher education." Charged with the task of assessing the state of humanities in higher education, Bennett reports the "disturbing" facts that "the humanities, and particularly the study of Western civilization, have lost their central place in the undergraduate curriculum," and that in the majority of the colleges and universities a student can obtain a bachelor's degree without having studied European history, American literature, or the civilizations of Greece and Rome.[26] According to Bennett, respect for diversity in education is "a good thing. But our eagerness to assert the virtues of pluralism should not allow us to sacrifice the principle that . . . each college and university should recognize and accept its vital role as a conveyor of the accumulated wisdom of our civilization. We are a part of and a product of Western Civilization."[27] According to Bennett, higher education institutions have the right and responsibility for deciding what their graduates should know, however, the decision should be based on the standard that "some things are more important to know than others." For him, "since we are the inheritors of Western civilization, students should have a deep understanding of its origins and development, from antiquity to the present, and a deep understanding of "a single non-Western culture than a superficial taste of many."[28]

In 1987, Allan Bloom's *The Closing of the American Mind* stirred great controversy among college students and educators across the country. For some, Bloom's book is a nostalgic celebration of the western classics through an attack on relativists, feminists, and organized minority students protests, among many others, who made their way into academia through the 1960s wave of social and political activism. As the title of the book suggests, the net effect of this has been the closing of the American mind: "higher education has failed democracy and impoverished the souls of today's students." Bloom's message is a call for a return to the study of Greek and Roman classics to infuse the curriculum with its original mission of teaching students the pursuit of the "first causes of all things. [29] He complaints that

> None of this concerns those who promote the new curriculum. The point is to propagandize acceptance of different ways, and indifference to their real content is as good a means as any.... Practically all that young Americans have today is an insubstantial awareness that there are many cultures, accompanied by a saccharine moral drawn from that awareness: We should all get along. Why fight?[30]

According to Bloom, faculty, administrators, and students of the 1960s are responsible for the failure of higher education to protect democracy and for impoverishing the mind and souls of the students. Having capitulated to the demands of student protestors, the faculty and administrators designed and implemented curricular reforms oriented to please the students' self-centered and self-defined "relevancy" and "critical thinking" view of teaching and learning. In Bloom's words, "Nothing that was not known to or experienced by those who constituted the enormous majority—which is ultimately the only authority in America—had any reality. Catering to democracy's most dangerous and vulgar temptations was the function of the famous 'critical philosophy.'"[31]

The publication of Bennett's and Bloom's work was followed by a systematic attack on multiculturalism by conservative scholars and writers. For instance, journalist Lawrence Auster in his 1987 book *The Path to National Suicide: An Essay on Immigration and Multiculturalism*, warns against uncontrolled immigration from non-western and third-world countries. In his view, the continuing massive migration of people from underdeveloped countries has destroyed the country's "sense of common citizenship" and "equality." Confronted with this reality, "clerics" of multiculturalism and diversity have conceived "the fantastic notion that we can achieve equality and unlimited diversity at the same time." In dealing with the inevitable inequality arising from cultural pluralism, the state has been activated to repress and control "speech dealing with racially sensitive subjects," "to grant privileges based on ethnicity," and to enforce the use of "racial quotas" in more and more areas of society.³² In *Profscam: Professors and the Demise of Higher Education* (1988), magazine writer Charles J. Sykes offers an indictment of what he perceived as some of the major wrongdoings going on in colleges and universities across the country. Sykes tries to show that professors are overpaid and underworked, they are bad teachers, they produce worthless research, and they dilute the liberal arts curriculum. The net effect of this for students has been watered-down courses, and worthless bachelor's degrees. Sykes' solution: colleges and universities should be reformed by eliminating research requirement for most professors, abolishing tenure, and centering the undergraduate curriculum on the Canon.³³ A similar indictment came from Roger Kimball in his book *Tenured Radicals: How Politics Corrupted Our Higher Education* (1990). Kimball's book represents an attack on the prevalence and dominance of issues of "race, gender, and class" in most higher education courses, which he sees as a distortion of the fundamental commitment of the university with the classical liberal arts curriculum. The people behind this problem are the "children of the sixties" who became professors and deans and who did not abandon their radicalism. Instead, they use their academic positions to "impose the politics and mind-set of the sixties by fiat."³⁴ In the same vein, Dinesh D'Souza's *Illiberal Education: The Politics of Race and Class on Campus* (1991) D'Souza echoes the romantic view of higher education expressed by Bennett, Bloom and their followers, when he describes the university as a scholarly community where professors and students walk around "talking of Proust and Michelangelo." According to D'Souza, this classical tradition has almost been destroyed primarily by policies to enforce affirmative action and multiculturalism. In doing so, college administrators have fostered a culture of victimization in higher education which corrupts and threatens to destroy "the highest ideals of liberal education." Although intended to compensate for historical injustices, these policies have created new forms of injustice in college campuses, not just because of discrimination against White students who are not admitted due to racial preferences being applied to Blacks and Hispanics, but also because of the recruitment of Black and Hispanic students who cannot academically compete with better qualified White, Jew, and Asian students. In D'Souza's opinion, the use of special admission policies, particularly at some of the most prestigious universities, explains the relatively high dropout rates of Blacks and Hispanics. Alternatively, in some universities the traditional curriculum has been reformed and diluted to meet the academic deficiencies and multicultural needs of students admitted under preferential admission programs.³⁵

Media coverage of the attack on multiculturalism aggravated its already precarious academic and professional appeal. For instance, from 1980 to

1985 *The New York Times* reported seven news stories all of which had to do with multiculturalism in Australia and Canada. However, from 1986 to 1991 the newspaper contained twenty-four articles dealing with multiculturalism in the United States and the conflicts it has created on college campuses. Based on anecdotes of political correctness and multicultural conflicts on college campuses, the media reinforced the entanglement of multiculturalism with issues of politically correct language, affirmative action, feminism, and sexual orientation. Hence, by the mid-1990s, multiculturalism had become an umbrella term representing a political alliance between oppressed racial and ethnic minorities, women, and members of the LGBTQ community. Writing for the *U.S. News and World Report*, John Leo labeled defenders of multiculturalism the "academy's new ayatollahs," and the "representatives of the P.C. clergy" who use their authority to silence the unconverted. Fred Siegel in an article for *The New Republic* refers to multiculturalism as a "cult" and a "new orthodoxy" which postulates an "all powerful 'Establishment' out to crush racial minorities, women, and the poor."[36] Similar attacks appeared in widely read magazines such as *The Atlantic Monthly*, *Harpers*, and *Time Magazine*.[37]

Finally, the attack on multiculturalism made its way into the internet during the early 2000s with the posting of the Ayn Rand Institute's (ARI) newsletter "Multiculturalism: The New Racism." In it, a series of contributing scholars chastise multiculturalists for their attempt to demonize Christopher Columbus, promoting the use of affirmative action policies and racial quotas, and Black female activists for demanding a return to tribalism. Furthermore, the ARI indicts ex-president Clinton's call for a Congressional formal apology for slavery. Alternatively, the ARI calls for a return to the values that have made the West and by extension the American culture "objectively" the best culture ever created: individualism, reason, individual rights, science and technology. In their view, these values, which represent the "backbone" of our civilization, have been eroded and corrupted by multiculturalists and academics who insist that "nothing is objectively better than anything else."[38]

By the late 1990s the opponents of multiculturalism had succeeded in their attempt at linking multiculturalism with the already inflammatory and unpopular notions of affirmative action and political correctness. In his 1991 commencement address at the University of Michigan President George W. Bush blamed advocates of "political correctness" for the atmosphere of "intimidation," "inquisition," "censorship" and "bullying" on some college campuses. In order to protect the rights of minorities and women, President Bush argued, intimidation and political correctness have declared "certain topics off-limits."[39]

The open attack on multiculturalism and diversity did not go unchallenged. In 1991, a group of educators formed the Teachers for a Democratic Culture (TDC) to launch a counteroffensive against conservative traditionalists particularly Lynne Cheney and her followers at the National Endowment for the Humanities (NEH). The TDC issued press releases and a newsletter, *Democratic Culture*, with the goal of exposing the myths and political motivations behind some highly publicized cases of alleged abuses of freedom of speech or discrimination by "left-wing and politically correct professors and administrators." Some of the cases include: the case of Cynthia Griffin Wolff against MIT for alleged professional, political, and sexual harassment; the financial involvement of the conservative Olin Foundation in the accreditation of colleges and universities; Professor Camille Paglia's attack on feminism; and Dinesh D'Souza's claim that most universities have been besieged by tenured radicals and affirmative action crusaders.[40]

In 2016, while addressing a large audience at Orient College, D'Souza told the group: "To me, this diversity game is a little bit rigged. . . . There's so much emphasis on racial diversity, gender diversity, transgender diversity and the most important type of diversity, intellectual diversity? A little bit scarce." D'Souza's position contrasts with that of a student who attended D'Souza's presentation and who told the school paper that "It was very rewarding to see students engaged in a respectful and challenging manner. . . . It's opened a door of discussion that we must continue and having a speaker present doesn't have to be the only moment when we have these conversations."[41] Perhaps we have entered or are getting closer to enter a new era of racial and ethnic relations in the United States. This is the promise of interculturalism!

NOTES

1. James Boyer, "Multicultural Education: From Product to Process," (College Park, MD: ERIC Document Reproduction Service) 1983, ED240224. See also, Paula Rothenberg. "Beyond the Food Court: Goals and Strategies for Teaching Multiculturalism." *Feminist Teacher* 13, no. 1 (2000): 61–73. http://www.jstor.org/stable/40545932.

2. James Bank, "Multiethnic Education in the U.S.A.; Practices and Promises," in (ed) Trevor Corner, *Education in Multicultural Societies*, (New York: St. Martin's Press), 1984, p. 79.

3. Carl A. Grant and Judyth M. Sachs, "Multicultural Education and Postmodernism: Movement Toward a Dialogue." In (ed) Barry Kanpol and Peter McLaren, *Critical Multiculturalism: Uncommon Voices in a Common Struggle*, (Connecticut: Bergin and Garvey), 1995, p. 93.

4. American Association of Colleges for Teacher Education, *Multicultural Teacher Education: Preparing Educators to Provide Educational Equity*, ed. H.

Prentice Baptise, Jr., Mira L. Baptise, and Donna M. Gollnick (Washington, DC: AACTE), 1980, p. 2–3.

5. Carl A. Grant and Judith M. Sachs, "Multicultural Education and Postmodernism," pp. 94–95.

6. Ibid., p. 94.

7. Peter McLaren, "White Terror and Oppositional Agency: Towards a Critical Multiculturalism." (ed) David Theo Goldberg, *Multiculturalism: A Critical Reader*, (Cambridge, MA: Blackwell), 1994, p. 48.

8. St. Clair Drake, "What Happened to Black Studies," (ed) Nathaniel Norment, Jr., *The African American Studies Reader*, (North Carolina: Carolina Academic Press), 2007, p. 338.

9. Paulo Freire, *Pedagogy of the Oppressed*. (New York: Herder and Herder) 1970.

10. Ibid., p. 46.

11. Ibid., p. 61.

12. In Peter McLaren, *Multiculturalism: A Critical Reader*, p. 59.

13. Henry A. Giroux, "Insurgent Multiculturalism," (ed) David Theo Goldberg, *Multiculturalism: A Critical Reader*, (Cambridge, MA: Blackwell), 1994, p. 328.

14. Charles Taylor, "The Politics of Recognition," (ed) David Theo Goldberg, *Multiculturalism: A Critical Reader*, (Cambridge, MA: Blackwell), 1994, pp. 100–101.

15. Ibid., p. 98.

16. Kymlicka, Multicultural Citizenship, p. 76.

17. Milton M. Gordon, *Assimilation in American Life: The role of race, religion and national origins.* (New York: Oxford University Press) 1964, pp. 151–152.

18. Will Kumlicka, "Liberal Complaciencies," (ed) *Is Multiculturalism Bad for Women*," (New Jersey: Princeton University Press) 1999, p. 31.

19. Ibid., p. 152.

20. Brian Walker, "Plural Cultures, Contested Territories: A Critique of Kymlicka." *Canadian Journal of Political Science*, Vol. 30, No. 2, June 1997, pp. 211–234, p. 222.

21. Yasmeen Abu-Laban and Daiva Stasiulis, "Ethnic Pluralism Under Siege: Popular and Partisan Opposition to Multiculturalism," *Canadian Public Policy*, Vol. 18, No. 4, December 1992, p. 368.

22. Ibid., p. 368.

23. Susan Miller Okin, "Feminism and Multiculturalism: Some Tensions," *Ethics*, Vol.108, No.4, July 1998, p. 682–683.

24. Sarah Song, "Majority, Multiculturalism, and Gender Equality," *American Political Science Review*, Vol. 99, No. 4, November 2005, p. 473.

25. Ibid., p. 486.

26. William Bennett, *To Reclaim a Legacy: A Report on the Humanities in Higher Education*. (Washington, DC: National Endowment for the Humanities), 1984, p. 2.

27. Ibid., p. 38.

28. Ibid., p. 13.

29. Ibid., p. 35.

30. Allan Bloom, *The Closing of the American Mind: How Higher Education has Failed Democracy and Impoverished the Souls of Today's Students*. (New York: Simon and Schuster) 1987, p. 377.

31. Ibid., p. 319.

32. Lawrence Auster, *The Path of National Suicide: An Essay on Immigration and Multiculturalism*, (West Virginia: Old Line Press, Inc.) 1987, p. 61–62.

33. Charles J. Sykes, *ProfScam: Professors and the Demise of Higher Education*, (Wisconsin: Reardon and Walsh) 1988.

34. Roger Kimball, *Tenured Radicals: How Politics Has Corrupted our Higher Education*," (New York: Harper and Row) 1990, p. 68.

35. Dinesh D'Souza, *Illiberal Education: The Politics of Race and Sex on Campus*, (New York: The Free Press), 1991, pp. 229–257.

36. See, *The New York Times*, "The Nation; Out of the Closet, Into the University," December 30, 1990; *The New York Times*, "The Nation: A Campus Forum on Multiculturalism; Opening Academia Without Closing it Down." December 9, 1990; *U.S. News and World Report*, "The Academy's New Ayatollahs: Politically Correct on Campus," December 10, 1990, p. 22.

37. For a chronology of published articles dealing with the controversy about multiculturalism and P.C. language see Debra Schultz, "To Reclaim a Legacy of Diversity: Analyzing the Political Correctness" Debates in Higher Education." (New York: National Council for Research on Women) 1993. (College Park, MD: ERIC Document Reproduction Service) 1979, ED 364170.

38. Ayn Rand Institute, *Multiculturalism: The New Racism*, (CA) http://www.aynrand.org/site/DocServer/newsletter_multiculturalism.pdf?docID=162 (accessed December 17, 2008).

39. *The New York Times*, "Bush Sees Threat to flow of Ideas on U.S. Campuses," May 5, 1991.

40. John K. Wilson (ed), *Democratic Culture: Newsletter of Teacher for a Democratic Culture*, Vol. 1–3, 1992–1994 (College Park, MD: ERIC Document Reproduction Service) 1983, ED377780.

41. Sarah Drumm, "Dinesh D'Souza speaks on race, political correctness," *The Bowdoin Orient*, November 4, 2016, v.146. (accessed January 22, 2019).

Chapter Six

Bridging Cultures: The Emergence of Interculturalism

Between 2006 and 2008, the Council of Europe, composed of forty-seven member states, surveyed politicians, and religious and migrant community leaders regarding their views on a variety of issues, including migration, intercultural relations, democracy, and human rights. In their 2008 report—*White Paper on Intercultural Dialogue* (WPID)—the Council of Europe declared that "The responses to the questionnaires sent to member states, in particular, revealed a belief that what had until recently been a preferred policy approach, conveyed in shorthand as "multiculturalism" had been found inadequate."[1] In 2010, German Chancellor Angela Merkel declared multiculturalism a complete failure. In her words, "Of course the tendency had been to say, 'Let's adopt the multicultural concept and live happily side by side, and be happy to be living with each other.' But this concept has failed and failed utterly."[2] Other politicians had expressed a similar view of multiculturalism as well as a pessimistic view of the political and cultural future of European societies unless multicultural policies were replaced with assimilationists policies.[3]

In her book, *The Crisis Of Multiculturalism In Europe*, Professor Rita Chin traced the roots of the failure and death of multiculturalism in Europe to a chain of interrelated economic, political, and cultural events that threatened the stability of Europe; for instance, the economic crisis of the 1970s made visible the vulnerability and economic disadvantage of ethnic minorities, and Ayatollah Ruhollah Khomeini's sentencing to death of Salman Rushdie for his book, *The Satanic Verses*, and the threat of terrorist attacks signaled the rise of religious and cultural intolerance. Furthermore, the increasing numbers of refugees and immigrants, arriving particularly from predominantly Muslim countries, sparked worries about national unity. Similarly, ethnic riots and police brutality in minority neighborhoods made evident the lack of structural and cultural integration across Europe.[4] Confronted with these challenges, some European governments developed multicultural policies that recognized the right of ethnic minorities communities to maintain their own cultural identity, and which granted political authority and power to their local community leaders, specifically to their male leaders. Critics of state-sponsored multiculturalism have suggested that these ". . . attempts at implementing multiculturalism . . . had the unintended effect of producing a more fragmented" society, as well as reinforcing the patriarchal and exploitative structures in certain ethnic communities[5]; however, Professor Chin argued that "Declaring multiculturalism 'dead' is a way of white Britons, Germans, and French telling immigrants, "We don't recognize you; you aren't a part of our society."[6] Despite the alleged policy shortcomings of multiculturalism, she continued, "the concept itself opened up a space in which to grapple with the place of immigrants and their cultural differences."[7]

INTERCULTURAL DIALOGUE AS A TOOL FOR CONVIVIALITY

As mentioned above, in 2008, the Council of Europe presented its WPID report at its 118th Ministerial Meeting in Strasbourg. The Council of Europe was founded in 1949 to promote the political, legal, and economic integration of the European countries. The WPID provides a policy-based framework for understanding and promoting intercultural dialogue, and for effectively and democratically managing diversity.[8] Although vaguely defined, intercultural dialogue refers to the open and respectful exchange of views among people who come from different cultural, religious, and political backgrounds. The WPID emphatically argues, on behalf of the governments it represents, that our common future depends on our ability to safeguard and develop human rights—as enshrined in the European Convention on Human Rights—democracy, and the rule of law, and to promote mutual understanding. It reasons that the intercultural approach offers a forward-looking model for managing cultural diversity. It proposes a conception based on individual human dignity (embracing our common humanity and common destiny). If there is a European identity to be realized, it will be based on shared fundamental values, respect for common heritage, and cultural diversity, as well as respect for the equal dignity of every individual. Intercultural dialogue has an important role to play in this regard. It enables us to prevent ethnic, religious, linguistic, and cultural divides, to move forward together, to deal with our different identities constructively and democratically, on the basis of shared universal values.⁹

Intercultural dialogue is only possible, however, if cultural diversity is democratically managed, participatory citizenship is strengthened, intercultural competencies are taught, and if people have access to spaces for engaging in intercultural dialogue. Below is a summary of the WPID's principles and conditions for effective intercultural dialogue.¹⁰

- Ethnic, cultural, religious, or linguistic affiliations or traditions cannot be invoked to prevent individuals from exercising their human rights, or from responsibly participating in society. Human rights abuses, such as forced marriages, "honor" crimes, or genital mutilation can never be justified, whatever the cultural context. Equally, the rules of a real or imagined "dominant culture" cannot be used to justify discrimination, hate speech, or any form of discrimination on the grounds of religion, race, ethnic origin, or other identity.
- The individual as a human being must be respected, as must be reciprocal recognition, in which this status of equal worth is recognized by all, and impartial treatment, where all claims arising are subject to rules that all can share. Unlike multiculturalism, however, interculturalism embraces a common core value system, which leaves no room for moral relativism.
- Gender equality is an integral part of human rights, and sex-based discrimination impedes the enjoyment of human rights and freedoms. Respect for women's human rights must be a non-negotiable foundation of any discussion of cultural diversity. Common gender experiences can overlap communal divides precisely because no community has a monopoly on gender equality or inequality.
- The barriers, such as language, racism, xenophobia, intolerance, discrimination, poverty, and exploitation, that prevent intercultural dialogue must be combated.
- Civil society and religious institutions share a common concern in promoting and protecting human rights, democratic citizenship, peace, dialogue, education, and solidarity. It is the responsibility of the religious communities themselves, through interreligious dialogue, to contribute to an increased understanding between different cultures. Apart from the dialogue between public authorities and religious communities, which should be encouraged, there is also a need for dialogue among religious communities themselves (interreligious dialogue).

INTERCULTURALISM IN THE UNITED STATES

As discussed in chapter 5, in the United States, signs of discontent with multiculturalism emerged in the mid-1990s.[11] Cornwell and Stoddard's words capture some of the main limitations of multiculturalism shared by its critics:

> The work done under the banner of multiculturalism sometimes treats cultures as if they have essential, traditional natures that are unified and unchanging. By characterizing cultures as multiple and discrete entities, the focus shifts away from the dynamics of cultural encounters. The paradigm of multiculturalism excludes the concept of dominant and subordinate cultures—either indigenous or migrant—and fails to recognize that the existence of racism relates to the possession and exercise of politico-economic control and authority and also to forms of resistance to the power of dominant social groups. Yet taking account of oppression should not result in presenting subordinate groups solely as victims; as Cathy suggests, we must also attend to the ways that less powerful groups resist the authority of the dominant culture.

Alternatively, Cornwell and Stoddard suggested the use of the term "interculturalism" to frame current discussions of interethnic and interracial identity, particularly in education:

> If today's students are to be prepared for citizenship and careers, they need to learn both about the complexity of their society and global interconnections. They can best understand the cultural pluralism within the United States by seeing it as one instance of the cultural changes, interactions, and multiplicities that make up human history. In order to comprehend the cultural diversities within and outside the United States under one rubric, we prefer the term "intercultural studies" over "multicultural," "diversity," "international," or "global." A relatively new term, it synthesizes the cross-cultural work of anthropology with the international studies of political science, area studies, and study abroad programs.

The intercultural approach proposed by Cornwell and Stoddard differs from the intercultural education model of the 1930s and 1940s by its global and interdisciplinary reach. It also departs from the multiculturalist concern with identity politics and "its monolithic views of the cultures being studied." Instead, interculturalists take a social-psychological approach to suggest that "a person's particular identity evolves in dialogue," rather than "by any single allegiance, category, or belonging." From this perspective, dialogue involves encountering and exploring cultural differences, and a willingness to critically examine our cultural heritage and practices in light of commonly accepted standards of human dignity and respect. Theoretically, intercultural dialogue "leads to a deeper understanding of the other's global perception."[12]

It also promotes a "valorization of policies, institutions, and activities which create common ground, mutual understanding and empathy, and shared aspirations."[13]

Ted Cantle, a major proponent of European interculturalism, sees the development of interculturalism as an opportunity to address some of the limitations of multiculturalism. Cantle's call for interculturalism includes:[14]

- Abandoning the old politics of identity and valuing what we have in common.
- Providing opportunities for intercultural learning so that people see others as an opportunity to learn, rather than as a threat.
- The contributions of faith should be valued, but if faith is in the public sphere, faith communities must also expect their views to be contested.
- Rejecting the use of identity politics to promote fear of other nationalities, faiths, and backgrounds to engender the loyalty of their own constituency or interests.
- Using social media to connect across old boundaries and to forge new international and intercultural relationships.
- Eradicating segregated environments that are totally impenetrable by outsiders, and in which communities live in fear of others.

In general, critics have argued that multiculturalists have failed in their attempt at creating a more inclusive and harmonious society by overemphasizing the importance of ethnicity in a person's identity. Identity-based multicultural policies, critics have countered, have contributed to the development of "separate communities within nation-states."[15] European interculturalists have worked with city planners, community organizers, academicians, and politicians to advance policies aimed at facilitating "immigrants' inclusion as much as possible and on devising policies concentrating on immigrants within the basic mainstream structure of public services."[16]

It is worth mentioning that, to a great extent, the inclusionist approach to interculturalism in Europe developed in response to the number of Muslim migrants that have been arriving in many European cities in recent years, sometimes perceived as a threat to the largest part of society. Zapata-Barrero described this form of intercultural policy intervention as follows:

> Assessment of city functions "through an intercultural lens" (education, the public domain, housing and neighbourhoods, public services and civic administration, business and the economy, sport and the arts); Urban safety; Mediation and conflict resolution; Languages; Media strategy; Establishing an international policy for the city; Evidence-based approach; Intercultural awareness training; Welcoming newcomers; and Intercultural governance (which includes partici-

pation and representation). These dimensions constitute a comprehensive range of different areas of intervention for ensuring the conditions to foster relations among people from different backgrounds, including national citizens.

THE INTERCULTURAL CURRICULUM: BRIDGING CULTURES

In the United States, much of the current work on intercultural education has centered around the work of Michael Vande Berg, who has developed a social-psychological approach for intercultural learning and intercultural competency development.[17] Author and scholar, Tara Harvey, has summarized Vande Berg's intercultural framework as follows:[18]

- Self-awareness. Learners must come into awareness of their cultural background and how that impacts their values, beliefs, and assumptions. Also, self-awareness must extend beyond a biographical understanding of the self to include an awareness of one's ways of making meaning, and of one's judgments, emotions, and physical sensations.
- Awareness of others. This competency refers to the importance of understanding and utilizing frameworks that can help make sense of cultural differences and similarities. It also involves coming into awareness of how others may make meaning of the world differently from us.
- Cultural bridging. The ultimate intercultural goal is to be able to bridge cultural differences. Meaning, bringing together competencies in the first three areas to shift perspectives, attune emotions, and ultimately, act in ways that are both appropriate and effective when living and working with people who are different from us.

Most multiculturalists would agree with Cantle's list of intercultural principles and with Zapata-Barrero's analysis of interculturalism. Both multiculturalists and interculturalists share a view of education as the institution to effect social change. They would agree that intercultural and multicultural curricula should be interdisciplinary, pluralistic, global, critical, and experiential. Moreover, both approaches assume that democracy "needs citizens who are both politically literate and capable of intercultural dialogue." Interculturalists have called our attention to the fact that "knowledge and understanding of other cultures can be achieved in many different ways both academically and experientially through dialogue."[19]

The micro social-psychological and dialogical approach proposed by interculturalists complements, rather than replaces, the multiculturalist macro sociological approach. As Tariq Modood has noted:

". . . interculturalists have made their own distinctive addition [to multiculturalism]: an emphasis on cultural encounters and everyday interaction in localities, schools, clubs, public spaces . . . Interculturalists have added the micro in terms of interpersonal cultural encounters and group dynamics at the level of youth clubs, neighborhoods, towns, and cities."[20]

Interculturalism offers a new model for bridging the cultural divide and for overcoming the limitations of state-sponsored interracial and interethnic ideologies and programs such as multiculturalism. It provides a holistic approach to ethnic and race dialogue, based on trust, empathy, and mutual respect. Whether interculturalism can bridge the cultural divide, only time will tell!

NOTES

1. Council of Europe. "White Paper on Intercultural Dialogue: Living Together As Equals in Dignity." https://www.coe.int/t/dg4/intercultural/source/white%20paper_final_revised_en.pdf (Accessed January 4, 2019).

2. Kate Connolly. "Angela Merkel declares death of German multiculturalism." *The Guardian*, October 17, 2010. https://www.theguardian.com/world/2010/oct/17/angela-merkel-germany-multiculturalism-failures (Accessed October 6, 2018). Ernesto Caravantes makes a similar argument regarding multiculturalism in the United States in his book, *From Melting Pot to Witch's Cauldron: How Multiculturalism Failed America*.

3. Ibid., p. 9.

4. Kenan Malik. *Multiculturalism and Its Discontents: Rethinking Diversity After 9/11*, (London: Seagull Books), 2013, p. 47.

5. In Rita Chin, *The Crisis of Multiculturalism in Europe: A History*, (Princeton: Princeton University Press), 2017, p. 269.

6. Ibid., p. 299.

7. Ibid., p. 300.

8. Berkley Center for Religion and Georgetown University. "Launch of White Paper on Intercultural Dialogue." berkleycenter.georgetown.edu/events/launch-of-white-paper-on-intercultural-dialogue (Accessed January 4, 2019).

9. Council of Europe. "White Paper on Intercultural Dialogue: Living Together As Equals in Dignity."

10. Ibid, pp. 19–22.

11. Grant H. Cornwell and Eve W. Stoddard. "Things Fall Together: A Critique of Multicultural Curricular Reform." *Liberal Education*, 80(4), pp. 40-51, Fall 1994.

12. Council of Europe. https://www.coe.int/t/dg4/intercultural/concept_EN.asp (Accessed January 3, 2019).

13. Katharina Bodirsky. "The Intercultural Alternative to Multiculturalism and its Limits." *EASA Workshop 2012, Working Papers*, 8, 2012. https://scholarworks.umass.edu/chess_easa/8 (Accessed December 11, 2018).

14. Ted Cantle (Community Cohesion and Intercultural Relations Professor). "About Interculturalism", tedcantle.co.uk/publications/about-interculturalism/ (Accessed January 2, 2019).

15. Ted Cantle. *Interculturalism: The New Era of Cohesion and Diversity*, (UK: Palgrave Macmillan), 2012, p. 53.

16. Alberto Zapata-Barrero. "Interculturalism in the post-multicultural debate: A defence." *Comparative Migration Studies*, 5(4), p. 10, 2017.

17. Barbara Kappler Mikk and Inge Steglitz. *Learning Across Cultures: Locally and Globally*, (NAFSA), 2017. See also Michael Vande Berg. "From the Inside Out: Transformative Teaching and Learning." Presented at the Workshop on Intercultural Skills Enhancement (WISE) Conference, February 3. (Wake Forest University), 2016.

18. See Tara Harvey. "Developing Intercultural Learning Objectives". Your Intercultural Teaching & Learning Home. https://www.truenorthintercultural.com/blog/developing-intercultural-learning-objectives (Accessed January 3, 2019).

19. Nussbaum. *Cultivating Humanity*, p. 82.

20. Tariq Modood. "Must Interculturalists Misrepresent Multiculturalism?" *Comparative Migration Studies*, 5(15), 2017, p. 6, .

Appendix A

Appendix A. Suburban Interracial Education Projects (1970)

Project Topic	Procedure
Preparing for Multi-Racial Classrooms	Training administrators and staff on multi-racial classroom teaching and learning, prejudice, Black Power, white parents' reaction, student discipline, etc.
Survey of Student and Faculty Attitudes Toward Minority Groups	Survey of students and faculty concerning misconceptions and misunderstandings about minorities. Provide lists of filmstrips and reading material for use in the classroom to face the problem.
Determining the Amount of Prejudice Held by Suburban Teachers	A survey of five essay questions: What will be the major problems at the school when the percentage of Negro students reaches at least one-fourth of the study body? What are the major problems of minority groups? Would you change your teaching procedures with minority groups present in your class? Should Black history be included in the school curriculum?
Survey of Three Suburban Kansas City, MO School Districts' Special Education	Questionnaires administered to students in their classrooms. Children brought the questionnaires to their parents; some questionnaires were mailed to parents. Sample questions: Would you fuss about sitting next to a black child? Would you object to living with a black family if you didn't have your own family? Items for parents: I would object to a black person using the same restroom that I use (Yes or No). Do you, personally, know any black person? I would like for my children to have a black teacher in school (Yes or No).

(continued)

Appendix A. (*continued*)

Project Topic	Procedure
Study Concerning How Prejudice is Reflected Through Responses to Dialect	Tapes were recorded of the typical dialect of Mexican-American, Negro, Oriental, German, and an individual possessing no dialect. Students listen to the tapes and answer a survey. Questions include: In what economic class would you place the speaker? How well educated do you consider this person?
In-Service Workshop Program	Use of self-evaluation tests about the person's knowledge of American-Negro Culture. Use of the filmstrip "Growing Up Black" to acquaint the educators with the realities of growing up black. Small group discussions.
Survey of Teaching Methods	Survey of teaching methods for improving intergroup relations. Do students have opportunities to learn democratic skills and values by interacting in problem-solving groups? Are the problem-solving groups concerned with real-problems in intergroup relations which are of immediate relevance to the lives of the students? Use of role-playing, sociometry, feedback analysis of group roles to improve interaction.
Improving Student Attitudes Toward Negroes	High school senior seminar to discuss the issue of open housing and what it means to be a Negro in America. Readings: *The Negro Revolt, Raisin in the Sun, Black Like Me,* and *The Autobiography of Malcolm X.*
Everybody has to be Somewhere	Survey of students' racial attitudes and their knowledge of Black Americans. Use the data to select and integrate material about Black people in history and culture courses.
Developing racial knowledge, understanding, and skills.	Curriculum: Use of ethnic pictures, stories, poems, films, filmstrips, textbooks, puzzles, puppets, the multiethnic game "See-Quees." Staff: Learning about paternalism, condescension, respect, stereotyping, slurs, and discrimination.
The Unaccepted Child in the Suburban Classroom	Use of large pictures and posters showing minority members, use of sociometric devices, and observations. To improve teacher's attitude, the project includes the use of study groups, counseling, and discussion of reading material on race relationships.
Curriculum Guide for Improving Classroom Human Relations	Use of human relations' knowledge and practice with any subject curriculum. Topics: history of Negroes and Mexicans, biography of notable Negroes and Mexicans, and myths about minority groups. Use of questionnaires to explore the problem of low self-concept among minority students.

Project Topic	Procedure
How to Implement Activities to Bolster Self-Concept	Personal conference and follow-up with mother. Praise for the child's improvement. Provide help through nurses, and teachers. Fitting curriculum to Negro student's needs.
Use of Music to Facilitate Acceptance of Ethnic Groups	Use of music resources such as *Music Across Our Country, Voices of America, Voices of the World, Music Sounds Afar,* and *Proudly We Sing.*
The Use of Poetry Written by Negroes as an Aid to Intercultural Understandings	Read Langston Hughes' poem "Refugee in America" to sixth-grade classes. Discuss the meaning of "refugee," "freedom," and "brotherhood." Tell the students that the poet was Negro. Tape the class discussion and study the tapes to categorize students' attitudes.
Contributions of Minorities in Math and Science	Use of a representative list of people, their contributions, and a partial bibliography. Students will prepare a bulletin board, will conduct oral and written reports and presentations.
Black Studies Unit for Eighth Grade	Segregation Experience: Dividing and granting the class arbitrarily using eye color, hair color, etc. and granting privileges to the majority group. Use filmstrips and short stories to explore stereotypes and myths about Black people. Distribution of "Fact Sheet About Black Americans."

Source: Joseph P. Caliguri (ed.), *Suburban Interracial Education Projects: A Resource Booklet.* (Missouri: School of Education and Division for Continuing Education, University of Missouri, Kansas City) 1970.

Appendix B

Appendix B. Western Regional School Desegregation Projects, 1971

Project Topic	Objective	Procedure
Motivating Change	To examine the function of the judicial processes as a motivator for local system change.	Use of *Mendez et al. vs. School District* to place the staff under desegregation political and time pressures similar to those they might experience in their local school district. Participants were presented with the *Mendez's* desegregation order. They had sixteen hours to take action and to provide a rationale for compliance or for their failure to comply.
Providing for Change: Staff Development	To train educators in identifying "targets" and "strategies" for change.	Identifying students' knowledge, teacher's feelings, teaching practices, peer relations, administrative relations, and community relations. Strategies: Audio-visual material, books, laboratory training, survey feedback, peer sharing, team formation, confrontation search, and problem-solving exercises.
Planning Change: Use of the Force Field Analysis	To use force field techniques to identify the forces pushing for stability and change in any local situation.	Using a Forces Field Analysis Chart to identify forces in favor and against desegregation within the local community.

Mark Chesler. *Preparing for School Desegregation: A Training Program for Intergroup Educators*, Vol.1, June 1972, p.11-12.

Appendix C

Appendix C.   American Indian Movement Activism, 1968-1979.

1968	AIM creates the MINNEAPOLIS AIM PATROL to address issues of extensive police brutality.
1969	AIM occupies ALCATRAZ ISLAND for nineteen months. AIM was there when United Indians of All Tribes reclaimed federal land in the name of Native Nations. First Indian radio broadcasts—Radio Free Alcatraz—heard in the Bay Area of San Francisco.
1969	INDIAN HEALTH BOARD of Minneapolis founded. This is the first Indian urban-based health care provider in the nation.
1970	LEGAL RIGHTS CENTER is created to assist in alleviating legal issues facing Indian people.
1970	AIM takeover of the abandoned property at the naval air station near Minneapolis focuses attention on Indian education and leads to early grants for Indian education.
1970	CITIZEN'S ARREST OF JOHN OLD CROW: Takeover of the Bureau of Indian Affairs' main office in Washington D.C. to show improper BIA policies. Twenty-four arrested for "trespassing" and released. BIA Commissioner Louis Bruce shows his AIM membership card at the meeting held after the release of those arrested.
1970	FIRST NATIONAL AIM CONFERENCE: 18 chapters of AIM convened to develop a long-range strategy for future directions of the movement.
1970	AIM assists the Lac Courte Oreilles Ojibwa in Wisconsin in taking over a dam controlled by Northern States Power which flooded much of the reservation land. This action leads to support by government officials and eventual settlement, returning over 25,000 acres of land to the tribe and providing significant monies and business opportunities to the tribe.
1972	RED SCHOOL HOUSE: the second survival school to open, offering culturally based education services to K-12 students in St. Paul, MN.

(continued)

Appendix C. (*continued*)

1972	HEART OF THE EARTH SURVIVAL SCHOOL: a K-12 school is established to address the extremely high drop-out rate among American Indian students and lack of cultural programming. HOTESS serves as the first model of community-based, student-centered education with culturally correct curriculum operating under parental control.
1972	TRAIL OF BROKEN TREATIES: A march on Washington, DC, ending in the occupation of BIA headquarters and resulting in the presentation of a 20-point solution paper to President Nixon.
1973	LEGAL ACTION FOR SCHOOL FUNDS: In reaction to the Trail of Broken Treaties the government abruptly canceled education grants to Heart of the Earth Survival School, Red School House and the Indian Community School of Milwaukee. Through successful legal action, the US District Court orders the grants restored and government payment of costs and attorney fees.
1973	WOUNDED KNEE 1973: AIM was contacted by Lakota elders for assistance in dealing with the corruption within the BIA and Tribal Council, which led to 71-day occupation and battle with the U.S. armed forces.
1974	INTERNATIONAL INDIAN TREATY COUNCIL (IITC): an organization representing Indian peoples throughout the western hemisphere at the United Nations in Geneva, Switzerland.
1974	WOUNDED KNEE TRIALS: This was the longest Federal trial in the history of the United States. The US District Judge Fred Nichol dismisses all charges due to government "misconduct" which "formed a pattern throughout the course of the trial" so that "the waters of justice have been polluted."
1975	FEDERATION OF SURVIVAL SCHOOLS is created to provide advocacy and networking skills to sixteen survival schools throughout the US and Canada.
1977	MIGIZI Communications founded in Minneapolis. The organization is dedicated to produce Indian news and information and educate students of all ages as tomorrow's technical work force.
1977	INTERNATIONAL INDIAN TREATY COUNCIL: establishes Non-government organization status within the United Nations in Geneva and attends the International NGO conference and presents testimony to the United Nations.
1977	AMERICAN INDIAN LANGUAGE AND CULTURE LEGISLATION: AIM introduces legislative language recognizing State responsibility for Indian education and culture. This legislation was recognized as a model throughout the country.
1978	FIRST EDUCATION PROGRAMS FOR AMERICAN INDIAN OFFENDERS: AIM establishes the first adult education program at Stillwater Prison in Minnesota. Other programs later established at other state correctional facilities modeled after the Minnesota program.

1978	CIRCLE OF LIFE SURVIVAL SCHOOL established on the White Earth Indian Reservation in Minnesota. The school receives funding for three years of operation from the US Department of Education.
1978	RUN FOR SURVIVAL: AIM youth organize and conduct 500-mile run from Minneapolis to Lawrence, Kansas, to support "The Longest Walk."
1978	THE LONGEST WALK: Indian Nations walk across the United States from California to DC to protest anti-Indian legislation calling for the abrogation of treaties. A tipi is set up and maintained on the grounds of the White House. The proposed anti-Indian legislation is defeated.
1978	WOMEN OF ALL RED NATIONS (WARN): established to address issues directly facing Indian women and their families.
1979	LITTLE EARTH HOUSING PROTECTED: an attempt by the US Department of Housing and Urban Development to foreclose on the Little Earth of United Tribes housing project is halted by legal action and the US District Court issues an injunction against HUD.
1979	AMERICAN INDIAN OPPORTUNITIES INDUSTRIALIZATION CENTER (AIOIC): creates job training schools to attack the outrageous unemployment issues of Indian people. Over 17,000 Native Americans have been trained for jobs since AIM created the American Indian Opportunities Industrialization Center in 1979.
1979	ANISHINABE AKEENG Organization is created to regain stolen and tax-forfeited land on the White Earth Reservation in Minnesota.

Adapted from *A Brief History of the American Indian Movement* by Laura Waterman Wittstock and Elaine J. Salinas http://www.aimovement.org/ggc/history.html (accessed February 21, 2009).

Appendix D

Appendix D. Ford Foundation Grants for Black Studies Programs, 1969

Black Studies Activities (Total $891,800)	Grants
Atlanta University Center Corporation: Collection and Cataloging of Papers of Martin Luther King, Jr., and other civil rights leaders	$85,000
National Endowment for the Humanities: Faculty Summer Institutes	$200,000
Association for the Study of Negro Life and History: Preparation of Afro-American materials.	$330,000
Frederick Douglas Institute of Negro Arts and History: Preparation of Afro-American materials.	$95,000
Atlanta University: Restoration and Inventory of university archives	$32,000
Fisk University: Restoration and Inventory of university archives	$24,200
Tuskegee Institute: Restoration and Inventory of university archives	$26,300
Southern Association of Colleges and Schools: Library acquisition for predominately Negro colleges	$99,300
Black Studies Programs (Total $883,533)	Grants
Howard University Black Studies Program	$143,567
Lincoln University Black Studies Program	$92,000
Morgan University Black Studies Program	$150,000
Princeton University Black Studies Program	$88,300
Rutgers University Black Studies Programs	$89,800
Stanford University Black Studies Program	$135,866
Yale University Black Studies Program	$184,000
Total=$1,775,333	

Source: Noliwe M. Rooks, *White Money, Black Power: The Surprising History of African American Studies and the Crisis of Race in Higher Education*, (Boston: Beacon Press), 2006, pp. 106–108.

Appendix E

Appendix E. Ford Foundation Grants for Black Studies-Related Programs at Selective Universities.

University	Department	Grants
Cornell University	Africana Studies and Research Center (1970)	1991: $261,643 1999: $250,000
Harvard University	African and African American Studies (1969)	1995: $250,000
Indiana University	African American and African Diaspora (1970)	1990: $300,000
Michigan State University	African American and African Studies (est. 1960s)	1990: $316,000 1991: $180,125
University of California, Berkeley	African American Studies (1970)	1991: $300,000 1999: $350,000 2000: $35,000
University of California, Los Angeles	Afro-American Studies (1969)	1988: $312,000 1999: $250,000
University of Michigan	Center for Afroamerican and African Studies (1966)	1988: $300,000
University of Pennsylvania	Center for Africana Studies (1966)	1991: $326,700
University of Virginia	Carter G. Woodson Institute for African-American and African Studies (1981)	2004: $300,000
University of Wisconsin	Afro-American Studies (1970)	1980: $300,000
Yale University	African American Studies (1969)	1969: $184,000 1989: $300,000

Source: Adapted from *Inclusive Scholarship: Developing Black Studies in the United States. A 25th Anniversary Retrospective of Ford Foundation Grant Making, 1982-2007.* (New York: Ford Foundation) 2007.
* Departments' names as to 2007. Year established in parenthesis.

Appendix F

Appendix F. Ford Foundation Grants for Minority Programs, 1968-1969 (Total=$44,140,400).

Programs Funded	Amount	Programs Funded	Amount
Minority Internships in State and Local Institutions	$710,000	Alaska Federation of Natives Charitable Trust	$175,074
Research and Action on Race, Poverty, and Social Behavior	$3,366,500	National Congress of American Indians Fund	$310,000
Higher Education for Disadvantaged Students	$949,591	Hearings on Mexican-American Affairs	$5,000
Attitudinal Research and Integration Studies	$517,953	Frederick Douglass Institute of Negro Arts and History	$175,074
Community Dispute Settlement	$257,776	Metropolitan Applied Research Center: Civil Rights Internships and expansion Conference on Equal Educational Opportunity	$738,000
Education for Clergy in Urban Problems	$607,500	Mexican-American Legal Defense and Educational Fund	$2,200,000
Human Relations Programs	$388,800	University of Notre Dame's Mexican-American Studies Program	$140,000
League of Women Voters Education Fund	$275,000	Organization for Business, Education, and Community Advancement	$19,830

(continued)

Appendix F. (*continued*)

Programs Funded	Amount	Programs Funded	Amount
Mass Media and Race Relations	$334,000	Southwest Council La Raza	$630,000 (1968) $21,595 (1969)
Metropolitan Funds	$657,500	A. Philip Randolph Educational Fund	$176,000
Project Bridge: Program to Change Attitudes	$225,000	N.A.A.C.P.	$378,000
Publications on Race and Education Affairs	$470,133	National Urban League	$1,480,000
Smithsonian Institution: The Poor People's March	$31,000	National Catholic Conference for Interracial Justice	$522,200
The Southern Courier Newspaper	$30,000	Research and Conference on Minority Employment (7 Institutions)	$820,018
Supplementary Surveys for Riot Commission	$640,000	Professional and Business Opportunity for Minorities (education, training, contracts)	$2,140,997
Experiments and Research in Legal Services for the Poor	$5,052,324	Puerto Rican Forum, Inc.: To establish a Loan Guarantee Fund	$250,000
NAACP Legal Defense Fund and Educational Fund	$750,000	Technical Assistance for Minority Business Development:	$2,036,693
Law School Development, Howard University, University of Mississippi	$965,147	Urban Affairs Foundation: For Internships With Minority-Group Politicians	$500,000
Central City Development	$900,000	Center for the Arts of Indian America	$150,000
Cleveland Community Programs	$902,240	National Indian Youth Council (Planning for Program Staff)	$27,500

Programs Funded	Amount	Programs Funded	Amount
Community Renewal Society, Chicago	$480,000	The Negro in Higher Education (Student and Faculty Training, Internships, Placement, Curriculum Changes, Faculty and Student Recruitment, Tutoring, etc.)	$8,724,470
Washington, DC: Rebuilding Riot-Torn Areas	$600,000	Improvement of Opportunities in Low-Income Areas	$2,888,611
Multi-Culture Institute, San Francisco (1969)	$200,000	University of Alaska: Conference on Indian and Eskimo Education (1969)	$56,500
Harvard University: (a) Research on de facto school segregation; (b) Research on effects of social change on children (1969)	(a) $800 (b) $34,614	New York City Board of Education: For Educational Reform (1969)	$30,000
		New York University: For Educational Reform	$44,000
Support of Journal *Integrated Education* (1969)	$30,000		
Cleveland area Human Relations curriculum (1969)	$125,000		

Source: *The Ford Foundation Annual Report, 1969*. https://www.fordfoundation.org/media/2439/1969-annual-report.pdf (accessed February 21, 2009).

Appendix G

Appendix G. Ford Foundation Grants for Mexican American Studies, Puerto Rican Studies, and Native American Studies, 1964 and 1979. (Total=$3,452,488)

Mexican American Studies (Total=$639,545)	
California State University, Northridge: Preparing Chicanos for Teaching Positions (1973-1976)	$471,270
University of California, Irvine Symposium on Chicano Psychology (1976)	$4,500
University of California, Los Angeles: Study of the Social, Economic, and Political Status of Mexican-Americans (1964-1966)	$648,000
Claremont University Center Establishing the Chicano Chronicle: A Newspaper of Mexican American History	$58,750
University of Notre Dame:	
Inter-Disciplinary Graduate Program in Mexican American Studies (1971)	$499,545
Analysis of Mexican American History (1968)	$140,000
Puerto Rican Studies (Total=$1,021,150)	
ASPIRA of America: Educational Program for Puerto Rican Youth (1972)	$260,000
Studies of the Migration Experience in Puerto Rico (1976)	$24,000
City University of New York: Center for Puerto Rican Studies (1973, 1979)	$737,150
American Indian Studies (Total=$609,273)	
University of Arizona: Graduate Program in American Indian Studies (1971)	$303,737
Boston University: Production of Educational Films About American Indians in the Southwest (1973, 1975)	$99,754
National Endowment for the Humanities: Fellowships for Sixteen PhD Candidates Preparing Dissertations on American Indians (1972)	$64,000
Navajo Community College: Preparation of Two Books Dealing With the Recent History of the Navajo People (1972)	$63,332
Oglala Sioux Community College Center (1972)	$78,450

Source: Bass Jack, *Widening the Mainstream of American Culture: A Ford Foundation Report on Ethnic Studies* (New York: Ford Foundation) 1978.

Appendix H

Appendix H. Survey of Ethnic Studies Programs and Years in Operation

Ethnic Program	Total N=760	Number of Programs	Average Years in Operation
African American Studies	264	California (53), New York (25), Illinois (17), Ohio (15), Washington (13), Pennsylvania (10), Massachusetts (9)	6.43
Mexican American Studies	124	California (57), Texas (10), Washington (10), Colorado (8).	6.40
Native American Studies	144	California (34), Washington (12), Wisconsin (9) Colorado(7), Minnesota (7)	5.50
Asian American Studies	71	California (33), Washington (9), Pennsylvania (4)	6.46
Jewish American Studies	49	New York (8), Pennsylvania (7), California (6), Ohio (6), Illinois (3), New Jersey (3), Wisconsin (3)	10.70
Puerto Rican Studies	41	New York (14), Illinois (4), California (3), Pennsylvania (3)	6.30
Slavic American Studies	32	Pennsylvania (7), Wisconsin (5), Ohio (4), Ilinois (3), North Carolina (3)	7.46
Italian American Studies	13	New York (5), California (1), Colorado (1) Connecticut (1), Illinois (1), Ohio (1), Pennsylvania (1), Texas (1), Wisconsin (1)	5.27
Irish American Studies	9	New York (2), Pennsylvania (2), Illinois (1), Kansas (1), Massachusetts (1), Ohio (1), Wisconsin (1)	4.63
Greek American Studies	7	Pennsylvania (2), Colorado (1), Illinois (1), Iowa (1), New Jersey (1), North Carolina (1)	4.40
Arab American Studies	6	Pennsylvania (3), California (1), Colorado (1), Washington (1)	4.50

Source: David E. Washburn, *Ethnic Studies in the United States: Higher Education*. Washington, DC: ERIC, 1981, (ED 206232). See also, Evelyn Hu-DeHart, *Ethnic Studies in U.S. Higher Education: History, Development, and Goals*. Washington, DC: ERIC, 1995, (ED382735).

Bibliography

Abu-Lughod, Janet L. 2007. *Race, Space, and Riots in Chicago, New York, and Los Angeles.* New York, NY: Oxford University Press.
Acuna, Rodolfo. 1972. *Occupied America: The Chicano's Struggle Toward Liberation.* San Francisco, CA: Canfield Press.
Adler, Mortimer J. *How to Read a Book: The Art of Getting a Liberal Education.* 1940. New York, NY: Simon and Schuster.
Adler, Mortimer, and Milton Mayer. 1958. *The Revolution in Education.* Chicago, IL: University of Chicago Press.
Astin, Alexander W., Helen S. Astin, Kenneth C. Green, Laura Kent, Patricia McNamara, and Melanie Reeves Williams. 1982. *Minorities in American Higher Education: Recent Trends, Current Prospects, and Recommendations.* San Francisco, CA: Jossey-Bass, Inc.
Auster, Lawrence. 1987. *The Path of National Suicide: An Essay on Immigration and Multiculturalism.* Monterey, VA: The American Immigration Control Foundation.
Bank, James. 1984. "Multiethnic Education in the United States: Practices and Promises." In *Education in Multicultural Societies*, edited by Trevor Corner, 68–95. New York, NY: St. Martin's Press.
Baptise, Jr., H. Prentice, Mira L. Baptise, and Donna M. Gollnick. 1980. *Multicultural Teacher Education: Preparing Educators to Provide Educational Equity.* Washington, DC: AACTE.
Baptiste, H. Prentice. 1980. *Multicultural Teacher Education: Preparing Educators to Provide Educational Equity.* Washington, DC: AACTE, 1980.
Bennett, William. 1984. *To Reclaim a Legacy: A Report on the Humanities in Higher Education.* Washington, DC: National Endowment for the Humanities.
Blake Jr., Elias, and Henry Cobb. 1976. *Black Studies: Issues in Their Institutional Survival.* Washington, DC: US Department of Health, Education, and Welfare.
Blauner, Robert. 1972. *Racial Oppression in America.* New York: Harper and Row.

Bloom, Allan. 1987. *The Closing of the American Mind: How Higher Education Has Failed Democracy and Impoverished the Souls of Today's Students*. New York, NY: Simon and Schuster.

Boody, Bertha M. 1926. *A Psychological Study of Immigrant Children at Ellis Island*. Baltimore, MD: Williams and Wilkins.

Boyer, James. 1983. *Multicultural Education: From Product to Process*. College Park, MD: ERIC Document Reproduction Service.

Bunzel, John H. 1969. "Black Studies at San Francisco State." In *Confrontation: The Student Rebellion and the Universities*, edited by Daniel Bell and Irving Kristol, 22–44. New York, NY: Basic Books.

Cantle, Ted. 2012. *Interculturalism: The New Era of Cohesion and Diversity*. New York, NY: Palgrave Macmillan.

Caravantes, Ernesto. 2010. *From Melting Pot to Witch's Cauldron: How Multiculturalism Failed America*. Lanham, MD: Hamilton Books.

Carmichael, Stokely, and Charles Hamilton. 1967. *Black Power: The Politics of Liberation in America*. New York: Random House.

Chin, Rita. 2017. *The Crisis of Multiculturalism in Europe: A History*. Princeton, NJ: Princeton University Press.

Cloward, Richard A. and Lloyd E. Ohlin. 1960. *Delinquency and Opportunity: A Theory of Delinquent Gangs*. New York: Free Press.

Cohen, Albert K. 1955. *Delinquent Boys: The Culture of the Gang*. New York: Free Press.

Cornwell, Grant H. and Eve W. Stoddard. "Things Fall Together: A Critique of Multicultural Curricular Reform." *Liberal Education* (4): 40–51.

Cubberley, Ellwood P. 1919. *Public Education in the United States: A Study and Interpretation of American Educational History*. Boston, MA: Houghton Mifflin.

Davis, James A. 1960. *A Study of Participants in the Great Books Program*. Chicago, IL: National Opinion Research Center.

Delaney, David. 1998. *Race, Place, and the Law*. Austin, TX: University of Texas Press.

Dewey, John. *Democracy and Education*.1916. New York, NY: Macmillan Company.

Drachsler, Julius. *Democracy and Assimilation*. 1920. New York: Macmillan Company.

Drake, St. Clair. 2007. "What Happened to Black Studies." In *The African American Studies Reader*, edited by Nathaniel Norment, Jr., 338–350. North Carolina: Carolina Academic Press.

D'Souza, Dinesh. 1991. *Illiberal Education: The Politics of Race and Sex on Campus*. New York, NY: The Free Press.

Erskine, John. 1923. *The Delight of Great Books*. Indianapolis, IN: Bobbs-Merrill Company.

Fairchild, Henry Pratt. 1947. *Race and Nationality as Factors in American Life*. New York, NY: Ronald Press Company.

Fanon, Frantz. 1967. *Black Skin, White Masks*. New York: Grove Press.

Fanon, Frantz. 1963. *The Wretched of the Earth*. New York: Grove Press.

Freire, Paulo. 1970. *Pedagogy of the Oppressed*. New York, NY: Continuum Publishing Corporation.

Gebler, Leo, Joan W. Moore, and Ralph C. Guzman. 1970. *The Mexican-American People: The Nation's Second Largest Minority*. New York, NY: Free Press.

Giroux, Henry A. 1994. "Insurgent Multiculturalism." In *Multiculturalism: A Critical Reader*, edited by David Theo Goldberg, 325–343. Cambridge, MA: Blackwell.

Giroux, Henry A. 1994. "Insurgent Multiculturalism and The Promise of Pedagogy." In *Multiculturalism: A Critical Reader*, edited by David Theo Goldberg, 325–343. Cambridge, MA: Blackwell.

Glazer, Nathan. 2003. *We are All Multiculturalists Now*. Cambridge, MA: Harvard University Press.

Gollnick, Donna M. 1978. *Multicultural Education in Teacher Education: The State of the Scene*. Washington, DC: American Association of Colleges for Teacher Education.

Gordon, Milton M. 1964. *Assimilation in American Life: The Role of Race, Religion and National Origins*. New York, NY: Oxford University Press.

Grant, Carl A., and Judyth M. Sachs. 1995. "Multicultural Education and Postmodernism: Movement Toward a Dialogue." In *Critical Multiculturalism: Uncommon Voices in a Common Struggle*, edited by Barry Kanpol and Peter McLaren, 89–105. Westport, CT: Bergin and Garvey.

Griffin Farah, Jasmine. 2007. *Inclusive Scholarship: Developing Black Studies in the United* New York, NY: Ford Foundation.

Guzman, Jessie Parkhurst. 1952. *Negro Year Book: A Review of Events Affecting Negro Life*. New York, NY: WM. H. Wise.

Harlem Youth Opportunities Unlimited, Inc. 1964. *Youth in The Ghetto: A Study of The Consequences of Powerlessness and a Blueprint for Change.* New York, NY: HARYOU.

Hunter, William A. 1980. *Multicultural Education Through Competency-Based Teacher Education*, Washington, DC: AACTE.

Illich, Ivan. 1970. *Deschooling Society*. New York, NY: Harper & Row.

James, Henry. 1968. *The American Scene*. Bloomington, IN: Indiana University Press.

Kidwell, Clara Sue and Alan Velie. 2005. *Native American Studies*. Lincoln, NE: University of Nebraska Press.

Kilpatrick, William Heard. 1947. *"Basic Principles in Intercultural Education."* In *Intercultural Attitudes in the Making; Parents, Youth Leaders, and Teachers at Work*, edited by William H. Kilpatrick and William Van Til, 2–4. New York, NY: Harper and Brothers.

Kimball, Roger. 1990. *Tenured Radicals: How Politics Has Corrupted our Higher Education*. New York, NY: Harper and Row.

Kirkpatrick, Clifford. 1926. *Intelligence and Immigration*. Baltimore, MD: Williams and Wilkins.

Kjolseth, Rolf. 1972. "Bilingual Education Programs in the United States: For Assimilation or Pluralism?" In *The Language Education of Minority Children*, edited by Bernard Spolsky, 2–10. Rowley, MA: Newbury House

Kymlicka, Will. 1999. "Liberal Complacencies." In *Is Multiculturalism Bad for Women?*, edited by Joshua Cohen, Matthew Howard, and Martha C. Nussbaum, 31–34. Princeton, NJ: Princeton University Press.

Lombardi, John. 1970. *The Position Papers of Black Student Activists*. College Park, MD: ERIC Document Reproduction Service.

———.1971. The President's Reaction to Black Student Activism. College Park, MD: ERIC Document Reproduction Service.

Malik, Kenan. 2014. *Multiculturalism and Its Discontents: Rethinking Diversity After 9/11*. London: Seagull Books.

Mazzei, Filippo. 1979. *Political and Historical Research on the United States of America*. Charlottesville, VA: University Press of Virginia.

McLaren, Peter. 1994. "White Terror and Oppositional Agency: Towards a Critical Multiculturalism." *In Multiculturalism: A Critical Reader*, edited by David Theo Goldberg, 45–74. Cambridge, MA: Blackwell.

Memmi, Albert. 1965. *The Colonizer and the Colonized*. New York: Orion Press.

Merton, Robert King. 1957. *Social Theory and Social Structure: toward the Codification of Theory and Research*. Glencoe, IL: Free Press.

Muse, Benjamin. 1968. *The American Negro Revolution*. Bloomington, IN: Indiana University Press.

Myrdal, Gunnar. 1962. *An American Dilemma: The Negro Problem and Modern Democracy*. New York, NY: Harper and Row.

National Advisory Commission. 1968. *Report of the National Advisory Commission on Civil Disorders*, Washington, DC: Government Printing Office.

Nussbaum, Martha. 1997. *Cultivating Humanity*. Cambridge, MA: Harvard University Press.

Okin, Susan Miller. 1998. "Feminism and Multiculturalism: Some Tensions." *Ethics* 108 (4): 682–683.

Reiss, Albert J. 1951. "Delinquency as the Failure of Personal and Social Controls." *American Sociological Review* 16, no. 2: 196. doi:10.2307/2087693.

Rojas, Fabio. 2007. *From Black Power to Black Studies: How A Radical Social Movement Became an Academic Discipline*. Baltimore, MD: John Hopkins University Press.

Rooks, Noliwe M. 2006. *White Money, Black Money: The Surprising History of African American Studies and the Crisis of Race and Higher Education*. Boston, MA: Beacon Press.

Ross, Edward A. 1914. *The Old World in the New: The Significance of Post and Present Immigration to the American People*. New York, NY: Century, Co.

Ross, Laura. 1998. *Inventing the Savage: The Social Construction of Native American Criminality* Austin, TX: University of Texas Press.

Ruberstein, Richard E. 1970. *Rebels in Eden: Mass Political Violence in the United States*. Boston, MA: Little, Brown and Company.

Shafali Lal 1973. "1930s Multiculturalism." In Walsh, John E. *Intercultural Education in the Community of Man*, edited by John E. Walsh, 1–19. Honolulu, HI: University of Hawaii Press.

Shapiro, Herbert. 1988. *White Violence and Black Response: From Reconstruction to Montgomery*. Amherst, MA: University of Massachusetts Press.

Smith, Paul Chaat, and Robert Allen Warrior. 1966. *Like a Hurricane: The Indian Movement from Alcatraz to Wounded Knee*. New York, NY: New Press.

Song, Sarah. 2005. "Majority, Multiculturalism, and Gender Equality." *American Political Science Review* (4): 473–489.

St. John Crevecoeur, John Hector. 1981. "Letters from an American Farmer." In *New World Metaphysics: Readings on the Religious Meaning of the American Experience*, edited by Giles B. Gunn, 134–35. New York, NY: Oxford University Press.

Sykes, Gresham M., and David Matza. 1957. "Techniques of Neutralization: A Theory of Delinquency." *American Sociological Review* 22 (6): 664. https://doi.org/10.2307/2089195.

Sykes, Charles J. 1988. *ProfScam: Professors and the Demise of Higher Education*. Washington, DC: Regnery Gateway.

Taylor, Charles. "The Politics of Recognition." 1994. In *Multiculturalism: A Critical Reader*, edited by David Theo Goldberg, 75–113. Cambridge, MA: Blackwell.

Thomas, R. Murray. 1965. *Social Class Differences in the Classroom: Social Class, Ethnic and Religious Problems*. New York, NY: David McKay Company.

Washburn, David E. 1974. *Multicultural Education Programs, Ethnic Studies Curricula, and Ethnic Studies Materials in the United States Public Schools*. College Park, MD: ERIC Document Reproduction Service.

———. 1981. *Ethnic Studies in the United States: Higher Education*. Washington, DC: ERIC Document Reproduction Service.

Wilson, John K. 1983. *Democratic Culture: Newsletter of Teacher for a Democratic Culture*. College Park, MD: ERIC Document Reproduction Service.

Zangwill, Israel. 1909. *The Melting-Pot: Drama in Four Acts*. New York, NY: Macmillan.

Zavella, Patricia. 1996. "Living on the Edge: Everyday Lives of Poor Chicano/Mexicano Families." In *Mapping Multiculturalism*, edited by Avery F. Gordon and Christopher Newfield, 362-386. Minneapolis, MN: University of Minnesota Press.

Index

Banks, James, 51, 86
Barbour, William W., 22
Battle, George G., 22, 43, 116
Belindo, John, 45, 54
Belle Isle Park, riot of 1943, 26
Bennett, William, 94, 96, 99, 131
Bilingual Education Act of 1968, 39
Black Arts and Cultures Series, 50
Black Muslims, 34, 43
Black Panther Party, 25, 34
Black Power Movement, 19, 25, 33–34
Blauner, Robert, 32, 33, 42, 123
Bloom, Allan, 87–88, 92, 124
Boody, Bertha M., 8, 21, 124
Boyer, James, 124
Boynton, Robert S., 70
Brown v. Board of Education of Topeka, 23–27, 34–36, 43, 46, 50, 55, 134
Bundy, McGeorge, 62, 63

canon, 46, 66, 82–83, 88
Cantle, Ted, 97, 100, 124
Caravantes, Ernesto, 4, 99, 124
Carmichael, Stokely, 33, 42, 124
Católicos Por La Raza, 38
Chavez, Cesar, 46
Chen, Dong L., murder of, 93
Cheney, Lynne, 98

Chin, Rita, 2, 93, 99, 124
civil disorders, 34–35, 42–43, 126
Civil Rights Act of 1964, 17, 28
Civil Rights Movement, 26, 34, 56, 71
Clark, Kenneth B., 29, 39, 50, 61, 64
Cloward, Richard, 38
Cohen, Albert, 38, 133
Colloquium on Important Books, 66, 68
Commission on Multicultural Education, 72
community colleges, ethnic studies programs in, 52–53
Compton, Arthur H., 14
Congress of Racial Equality, 32
Cornwell, Grant H., 96, 124
Cottier, Allen, 44
Council of Europe, 93–94, 99–100
critical multiculturalism, 78, 80–83
Cubberley, Ellwood P., 6, 20, 124
cultural deprivation, 46

Dewey, John, 74, 75, 78, 124
Dickerson, Earl B., 34
discussion groups, and the Great Books Movement, 69–71
Dornbusch, Sanford, 66
Drachsler, Julius, 10–12, 21, 124
Drake, St. Clair, 80, 124

D'Souza, Dinesh, 88, 90, 92, 124
DuBois, Rachel D., 20, 30, 55
Du Bois, W. E. B., 22, 27, 52

Edgerton, Henry, 35
Einstein, Albert, 22
Emerson, Ralph W., 13
Encyclopedia Britannica Films, 69
Erskine, John, 124
Ethnic Heritage Studies Programs Act, 47
ethnic studies, v, 2–3, 45–61, 63, 74, 76, 80, 119, 121, 127
Eurocentric curriculum, 46, 80

Fairchild, Henry Pratt, 124
Fletcher, C. Scott, 77
Ford Foundation, 2, 50, 54–56, 58, 61, 69, 111, 113, 115, 117, 119, 125
Franklin, John H., 34, 64
Freire, Paulo, 124
Fund for Adult Education, 69, 75
Fusco, Coco, 89

Gates, Henry Louis, 67
gender equality, 91, 95, 126
Giroux, Henry A., 76, 91, 124-125
Glazer, Nathan, 10
Goldblatt, Mark M., 65
Gordon, Milton, 34, 43, 125
Great Books Movement, 66, 68, 70, 72
Great Books, 14, 66, 68–72, 75–76, 124

Hamilton, Charles V., 41, 50, 132
Harvey, Tara, 106, 108
Haskell, Edward F., 72, 73, 82
Henderson, Vivian, 43
Hoffman, Paul G. 77
Hutchins, Robert M., 31, 74, 76

inclusion, 2, 48, 72, 82–83, 86, 97
insurgent multiculturalism, 76, 82, 91, 124–125
intercultural competencies, 95

Jackson, Robert, 66
James, Davis, 75, 76, 124
Javits, Jacob K., 54
Johnson, Lyndon B., 40, 44, 47, 51

Kallen, Horace M., 17, 29
Kellor, Frances A., 16, 17, 29
Kennedy, John. F., 46, 51
Kimball, Roger, 88, 92, 125
King, Martin L., 42, 50, 59, 119
Kymlicka, Will, 83–84, 125

Lewis, John, 42, 50

Malik, Kenan, 99, 125
marginal man, 3, 64, 74
Matza, David, 38
Mendez et al. v. Westminster School District et al., 27, 31, 113
Merkel, Angela, 11, 12, 101, 107
Merton, Robert, 38
Mikk, Barbara K., 108
Modood, Tariq, 107, 108
Morrison, Tori, 67

National Council for Accreditation of Teacher Education, 72, 78
National Opinion Research Center, 70, 75, 124
No One Model American, 72

Ohlin, Lloyd, 38
Okin, Susan 93, 99, 134
Olin Foundation, 90

Paglia, Camille, 98
Park, Robert, 34, 36, 67–69, 72, 98, 100, 132, 133, 135
People v. Chen, 85
Powell, James, 32, 40
pragmatism, 14–15, 66–67, 70

Reiss, Albert, 38
Roosevelt, Eleanor, 22, 33, 34
Rubenstein, Richard E., 32, 40

Santa Clara Pueblo v. Martinez, 85
Schweiker, Richard S., 45, 54, 55
Shulman, Harry M., 11, 82
Siegel, Fred, 89, 97
Song, Sarah, 85, 126
Standard for the Accreditation of Teacher Education, 72
Steele, Shelby, 59, 67
Steglitz, Inge, 108
Stoddard, Eve W., 104, 108, 132
Stonequist, Everett V., 11, 72, 82
Sumner, William G., 36
Sykes, Charles J., 88, 126
Sykes, Gresham M., 38, 96, 100, 134

Taylor, Charles, 83, 91, 126
Toscano, Hercella, 47
Turner, Frederick J., 13

Viva Kennedy Movement, 46, 51

Walker, Brian, 92, 99
Wallace, George, 24, 31
West, Cornel, 14, 15, 29, 67, 97, 100
White Paper on Intercultural Dialogue, 93, 99
White, William Allen, 22
whiteness, 80–82
Wirth, Louis, 11, 72, 73, 82
Wolff, Cynthia Griffin, 98

Zapata-Barrero, Alberto, 105, 108

About the Author

Alfredo Montalvo-Barbot is currently associate professor of sociology and department chair at Emporia State University in Kansas. He received his PhD in Sociology from Southern Illinois University in Carbondale, Illinois.

Made in the USA
Columbia, SC
27 December 2022

75077515R00086